CITIZEN
virtues

CITIZEN
virtues

A new pattern for living

DAVID ALTON

HarperCollins*Publishers*

HarperCollins*Publishers*
77–85 Fulham Palace Road,
Hammersmith, London W6 8JB

First published in Great Britain in 1999 by HarperCollins*Publishers*
10 9 8 7 6 5 4 3 2 1

A catalogue record for this book
is available from the British Library.

ISBN 000 274019 2

Printed and bound in Great Britain by
Creative Print and Design (Wales), Ebbw Vale

To Lizzie, Marianne, Padraig, Philip, James,
and my late parents

Contents

Introduction

'Is ar scath a cheile a mhaireann na daoine.'
It is in the shelter of each other's lives that the people live.

'Citizen' is a word which has lost a good deal of its original meaning. At its simplest level, the word means 'a member of a nation or other political community', but the concept of 'citizenship' goes further than that. *Collins English Dictionary* defines citizenship as 'the condition or status of a citizen, with its rights and duties'. We talk enough about rights, but what about duties? They seem to have gone out of fashion. Something similar has happened with the word 'virtue'. Once positively associated with strength, sacrifice, courage and valour, the concept of virtue has been radically devalued, coming to imply a wishy-washy, goody-two-shoes approach to life. With the loss of the real meaning of these two words, a vital balance has disappeared from our society.

A snapshot of contemporary Britain shows what happens when it is no longer deemed important to be a 'good citizen' and when the pursuit of true virtue is abandoned. Just look around you for the obvious signs:

- Isolated individuals in our cities
- Fractured community bonds
- Lack of participation in local and national government
- Elected representatives who abandon public service, driven by the desire for power or money
- Devaluation of personal commitments and promises: a 600 per cent increase in marriage breakdown over the last 30 years; one in five children see their parents divorce before they are 16

- Children abandoned by their fathers: 800,000 have no contact with their fathers; 64,000 are in local authority care; 46,000 are on child protection registers

- Many children watching TV for at least two hours a day, some for over five hours, much of it violent in nature

- 50 per cent of all crimes committed by those under 21; 10 times as many crimes committed now as in 1955; a crime rate which is 40 times that of 1901

- Schools plunged into crisis by crime, violence, truancy, low levels of literacy and numeracy, increasing numbers of children running away from home

- Loss of respect and care for the elderly: 1 million elderly people see no one during the course of an average week

- One in five pregnancies aborted; 100,000 human embryos destroyed annually in British laboratories; eugenics and euthanasia now practised openly; the sanctity of human life destroyed

- Illegal drugs taken each week by over a million young people; 160 babies born addicted to purified cocaine in one recent twelve-month period

This is a Britain which has emphatically lost its virtue and which has found a confused variety of worthless things to put in its place. What went wrong? Can we find a way out?

Winners and losers

We have never been more materially affluent and yet modern life seems less and less able to meet our expectations. We feel like losers even if we are judged to be winners in material terms.

Clinical depression is 10 times higher in people born after 1945 than among those born before 1914.[1] Women under the age of 35 are the most vulnerable – yet, surely, they have never been more liberated, never better able to succeed in life?

> *We have never been more materially affluent and yet modern life seems less and less able to meet our expectations.*

A Gallup survey revealed that compared with 30 years ago, when 28 per cent thought that they had become happier, only 7 per cent of those polled feel happier today – with 53 per cent believing that life is becoming unhappier. Often people feel afraid. We say this is a more permissive age, but many of the things which we were free to do as children – to play alone in the park or roam the countryside – we are no longer permitted to do. It is not safe. Society's expected order has broken down, and not just in terms of public safety. It begins with the family.

The great disruption

Francis Fukuyama says that 1967 was the year of 'the great disruption'.[2] He believes that the contraceptive pill and the sexual freedom it offers has undermined the family: the sacrifice required by faithful marriage is no longer required for sexual fulfilment.

Marriage is the most important of the community's institutions to crumble. This crumbling has been encouraged by faster and easier divorce – accelerated further in 1996 by the Family Law Act, with the abolition of 'fault' in divorce cases. If the Government had expended as much energy on finding ways to help couples stay together as they and the Law Commission invested in finding easier and quicker ways to enable marriages to break up, would the outcome have been more positive?

But divorce laws and the pill are not the only catalysts of family breakdown. There are other factors:

- A more cavalier attitude towards children – marriages are no longer held together 'for the children's sake'
- The massive influx of women into the workforce – in September 1997 there were for the first time more women working than men

- A welfare system which has institutionalized single parenthood and discriminated against the mother who chooses to
  live and work at home with her children

With such widespread family breakdown, young people are growing
up incapable of passing on to their own children the accumulated
treasures and values of the community, because this is something
they have never experienced.

Promise breakers and promise keepers

The undermining of binding promises in a family context has led to
a broader breakdown of care and obligation as individualism has replaced citizenship. Trust weakens as our covenant is severed with
our unborn children, our partners, our dependents, our aged relatives, our local community. In Washington, USA, in October 1997,
I saw some of the million men who stood on Capitol Hill and renewed their pledges as Promise Keepers. In itself this will not
guarantee faithfulness or provide an insurance policy against our
human frailties, but at least they were making an important statement of intent.

---

*We cannot go on acting solely as individuals
in isolation from everyone else.*

Likewise, true freedom and strong communities (the sort of society
we have lost today) can only be built up through self-discipline and
a sense of the common good. We cannot go on acting solely as individuals in isolation from everyone else. The thought, attributed to
Margaret Thatcher, that society does not exist, and that the world
is simply made up of freewheeling individuals, could not be more
dangerous or more wrong. Communities are dependent on the
relationships which we forge with others. We are all dependent on
each other. It is no irony to say that only by yielding something of
ourselves can we begin to function as true individuals living in community with others. Without shared rules, stable relationships,
fidelity and a willingness to serve others, we shrink into being

merely atomized individuals, invariably unhappy, unfulfilled and often alone.

Privatized lives

What might be called the 'virtuous path' is often there for us to follow, but how often do we avoid it and choose to go another, more selfish (and ultimately less rewarding) way? We have been indoctrinated into privatizing our lives, into showing little interest in the fate of everyone else. To reach out and help would be too big a risk of ourselves. And anyway, there is so much need, so many crises, what can we do?

I often feel like Robert Louis Stevenson's little boy who complains that 'the world is so big and I am so small; I do not like it at all, at all'. But then I remember that landslides happen when small stones start to move. We are those small stones.

It is impossible to live in watertight compartments, cut off from the rest of the world. Our personal and collective actions affect others. The choices which we make carry consequences, so why not make them positive ones?

Landslides happen when small stones start to move. We are those small stones.

Whether we like it or not, we come from a community, with all its faults and failings. Each of us, with all *our* faults and failings, has some gift to return to that community. This is how it should be. It is in the community that we will find fulfilment for our lives. Privatized lives lead to unhappiness: if we reach out in active citizenship, our fractured communities and broken individuals will be transformed.

The 1980s was a decade of unrestrained individualism. The common good was a discarded notion and men and women were encouraged to look after number one. The 1990s, however, may be remembered as the decade during which the common good began to reassert itself over self-interest.

The common good

Thomas Hill Green, a great nineteenth-century idealist, moral philosopher and exponent of ethical liberalism, held that virtue was best understood as a personal outpouring for the common good. 'And if the idea of the community of good for all men has even now little influence,' he wrote, 'the reason is that we identify too little with good character and too much with good things.'[3]

Whole centuries and cultures apart, Green shared with the Greek philosopher Aristotle a belief in virtuous activity as the greatest good. Green argued that Aristotle's list of virtues had been enlarged in modern times through Judaeo-Christian influences – especially through the concept of the 'brotherhood of man'. In the light of the age-old concept of the 'common good', he examined the two vital aspects of existence as a human being – as an individual object in the world and as a moral agent with the capacity to choose a better or worse path.

Green's Victorian Idealism, his belief in virtue, his hostility towards materialism, his love of community, are all back on the agenda now as we question the individualism of previous decades.

A stockholder society

During the 1980s citizenship was measured, if at all, not in terms of ethical choices or personal virtue, but in stocks and shares and property ownership. The idea took hold that self-interest alone is what motivates people. Why should anyone be interested in the common good? This was not a stakeholder society but a society of stockholders. Thatcherites justified their economic liberalism by quoting Adam Smith, the early nineteenth-century economist – but Smith never believed in unrestrained self-interest. Unlike modern 'liberals', Smith believed that market forces had to be tempered, that economic forces must sometimes be *restrained* through active intervention. The popular call today is for a 'stakeholder society'. If this involves such a tempering of the market and a more responsible view of personal and corporate citizenship, then we should welcome it.

New Labour, old Tories

So what is the situation today? The unrestrained liberal economics of the right have converged with the liberal social theories of the left. Thatcherite economics have been adopted by the Blair Government and are coupled with a rights-based agenda pushed primarily by the Lord Chancellor's Department (with the active collaboration of some Liberal Democrats). Both endanger the already fragile balance of civil society. When both economic and rights-based liberalism converge, the economically disadvantaged and the stability of the community are doubly threatened. Often the same people are hit twice.

The best way to challenge the political consensus which now predominates will be through constitutional reform:

- Scottish and Welsh devolution
- Directly elected mayors
- Reform of the House of Lords
- The likelihood of elections conducted under proportional representation

We must also encourage a return to good citizenship and the re-building of strong communities. There are signs of hope, but only if we *collectively* make the most of them and push for more.

Individuals in community

The individualism of the 1980s was a backlash against an overbearing State, which dominated the lives of millions of people for the greater part of this century. The strength which can come from the community was wrongly regarded by many as a dangerous first step towards State control. The result was that the baby was thrown out with the bath-water. It is possible, however, to build a balanced community, one based on a happy medium between extreme individualism and extreme collectivism.

We need to fight the defeatist belief that
because we sometimes fail it is better not to try at all.

When citizens mobilize themselves – individuals working in community – everyone benefits; even when mistakes are made, we should never give up. We need to fight the defeatist belief that because we sometimes fail it is better not to try at all.

Messy lives

There is not a man or woman among us who has not failed or made a mistake. The person who has never made a mistake has never made anything, as the saying goes. Do we then throw in the towel after the first set-back rather than risking another round? Communities are messy places inhabited by people just like us, all experiencing problems, uncertainties and failures. The pursuit of true virtue and the common good does not immunize a citizen against personal failure, but it does provide a framework in which to seek an ordered life and an ordered society where everyone is cared for and no one is left out in the cold. If every person plays their part – small stones making a landslide – progress will inevitably follow, despite mistakes along the way.

Death of a Princess

At the end of August 1997 the death of Diana, Princess of Wales triggered an introspective debate about 'what we are here for'. In Diana people could see great virtue but, like the fabled curate's egg, it was there only in parts.

In an often unfocused and inarticulate way, people seemed to sense that in the debris of a mangled motor car in a Paris underpass lay the clue to their own mortality and their own messed-up lives. With their dead Princess millions shared a desire to be more compassionate than 1980s Britain had allowed. Diana had shown compassion for others despite enormous personal difficulties. She did not subscribe to that defeatist belief that if failure threatens, it is better not to try at all.

Millions also understood that even for this icon of material attainment, all the possessions in the world had not prevented the unhappiness and loneliness which sprang from the breakdown of marriage and family life. Whatever a person's rank, when their family – the most basic community of all – is destroyed, it leads to terrible dysfunction.

A dysfunctional society

That dysfunction was underlined at a different level in 1995, when the headmaster Philip Lawrence was murdered outside his South London school; and in 1996 when 16 children and their teacher were gunned down in Dunblane. And who will ever forget the shock of learning, in 1993, that two 10-year-old boys from Liverpool had murdered two-year-old James Bulger? James's killers both came from dysfunctional families. An investigation of Philip Lawrence's killers revealed a similar absence of fathers and stable home life.

Moments like these in the life of a nation can turn into a welter of self-criticism. What has happened to our society? When did things start to go wrong? Who or what can we blame? Several writers warned that it could lead to 'moral panic' – although anything might be preferable to indifference and complacency.

Citizen virtues

In fact, the subsequent debate has been very constructive. The developing themes of the 1990s have been an interest in ethical behaviour and a gradual replacement of the self-indulgent language of rights and entitlements with a richer language of duties and responsibilities. The desire to be more compassionate sits very happily with these other two impulses. Tony Blair's 1997 election campaign intuitively and decisively homed in on these themes, although only time will tell how well the rhetoric squares with the reality. At least a pursuit of the common good appears to be back on the agenda. But what about the healing of other vital, but damaged, virtues? What about the pursuit of honesty in public life? How can a viable community or country exist without a backbone of trust?

Trust in me

It would be a mistake to forget that the economic record of the Conservatives was not what finally brought them down. It was the issue of trust. John Major was still perceived as a decent man, but his administration was not. As Tony Blair continues to utter his election call to 'trust us', he should ponder on the consequences for John Major of his Government's loss of political virtue. In the early stages, Tony Blair consciously modelled himself on President Bill Clinton – whose administration's loss of public trust should act as another stark warning to him.

No one in the Labour Government should underestimate the electorate's real desire for more virtuous government.

Some of the early omens suggest that the lessons of 'cash for questions' and the matter of public trust have not been fully understood:

- Geoffrey Robinson, the Paymaster General, took 'trust' to mean an offshore institution for investors.
- Formula 1 – with vested interests in tobacco advertising – put their trust in a huge donation to the Labour Party, which then had to be repaid.
- The arms industry trusted Robin Cook to renew export licences – to countries like Indonesia – and they were not disappointed.
- In the European and Westminster Parliaments, after discovering some untrustworthy Labour MPs voting against the Party line, the Labour Whips replaced trust with threats, coercion and finally deselection.

Some of this is merely a description of the inevitability of life after Midas – the fabled king who eventually lost his golden touch. But no one in the Labour Government should underestimate the electorate's real desire for and expectation of more virtuous government. Disappoint them and the result will be catastrophic for the Party but also, in the longer term, catastrophic for public confidence in our democratic institutions.

The previous Government was voted out because of a loss of trust, and Labour was voted into power in the hope of restoring that trust. The Government needs to understand the sense of relief which greeted the fall of the *ancien régime* and the high expectations of the voters. They should welcome with open arms these new and enthusiastic citizens, keen to find ways of being more compassionate, more responsible. They should allow them a free and active stake in their own community, and make the most of the new impetus for change and involvement.

Ancient truths

For each of us citizenship has to be experienced and learned. It does not simply consist of a series of theories. But this is not a new discovery and we would do well to remember the wisdom of earlier times.

Among the ancients, Aristotle is best known for his belief that everyone should pursue virtue, and for his upholding of communal existence, or *koinonia*. This *koinonia* was not about civic structures of government but about the qualities in mankind which made civic co-existence a possibility. In *Politics* he wrote that we are not like 'solitary pieces in chequers', but need to cultivate a common life. Shame, he said, would attach to those who privatized their lives and opted out of communal existence.

What was true for Athens was also true for Rome. Cicero, in his work *On Duty*, argued for active participation in the common life. He said 'the whole glory of virtue is in activity'.

The Roman senator Epictetus said that material achievements were overshadowed by the pursuit of good citizenship: 'He is highly valued by the state who raises not the roofs on its houses but the souls of its citizens.'

Contemporary political activity has too frequently been measured by the number of housing units constructed or by the economic output, and not by the strength of relationships and the quality of community life. Anyone who travelled in the former Soviet Union will recall the obsession which tour guides had with explaining the output of a model factory or a communal farm, while remaining silent when casually questioned about aspects of daily life. Nothing could be more soul destroying.

Aristotle, Cicero and many of the other ancients saw active engagement in the life of the community not as an optional extra but as a *duty*. Each citizen shared in the glories and the burdens alike. Withdrawal from the common life marked a person as a worthless good-for-nothing.

The shelter of each other's lives

My Irish-speaking mother came from the famine lands of the west of Ireland. There they have a saying which illustrates another strength of common life, and which appears at the beginning of this Introduction: 'It is in the shelter of each other's lives that the people live.' It diminishes us – we live less fully – when we are isolated from the life of the community. This spiritual deprivation is mirrored by the practical shelter and support which the community can offer in times of trial.

I was struck by the solace which grieving relatives drew from the respectful queue of people who had come to a tiny cottage in Clonbur, a village in Galway, where an elderly lady had died. The great gathering at a wake eases much of the grief and shock which is so destructive when a person is left to shoulder the burden alone. The destruction of community life has robbed us of meaningful lives and even comfort in death.

It diminishes us – we live less fully – when we are isolated from the life of the community.

Modern citizenship

A nation or community will not survive for long if its civil structures are decaying or if its rulers do not pursue civic virtues. But it is not only the rulers who need to change. A society which is individualized and where communities are fractured is living dangerously close to the edge. Each citizen must become the catalyst for change, the instrument of renewal. It cannot all be left to those 'in charge'. We are all responsible.

The purpose of this book is to examine the essential values which we have lost – much as a result of the pell-mell rush to individualism – and to suggest some practical ways in which a citizen might shoulder once again some of the community's duties. It is about rediscovering Green's sense of Idealism and the common good, Aristotle's belief in activity, and Cicero's belief in duty.

Liberal freedom too easily becomes the mere power of choice without obligation. When we exercise choice and choose one option over another out of self-interest, we may ultimately become less free. A more fundamental freedom occurs when a citizen chooses a course of action in the wider interest, for others, not self.

How a person acts as a moral agent affects everything from how they treat their environment and their neighbours to the pursuit of ethical standards in commerce or the shouldering of civic duties. It is not a spectator sport or the preserve of a few well-meaning specialists: everyone is part of the community; everyone is a citizen and can act. This book is not about definitions or theories. It is about how modern citizens striving to make a difference to their society can make sense of Aristotle's ancient virtues:

- Justice
- Wisdom
- Temperance
- Courage
- Magnanimity
- Tolerance
- Munificence
- Prudence
- Gentleness

That is why I have chosen to incorporate these virtues in the five themes of **responsibility**, **values**, **discernment**, **confidence** and **activity**. Virtue in its original sense is not an unrealizable objective. It is attainable through acts of personal and corporate responsibility, the upholding of ethical values, the exercise of discernment, and the confidence of our actions. The virtuous citizen will be responsible – not merely demanding rights but also aware of reciprocal duties. He or she will be prepared to put the common good before personal choice, will learn how to evaluate, and will be ready to make a stand, campaigning for vital change.

1/ Citizen Responsibilities

In this first chapter I want to look at the lopsided relationship between rights and responsibilities. In recent decades the emphasis has been all on rights – what am I due? Now, at last, we are beginning to wake up to our responsibilities again – what can I do? But we are still struggling with a lack of vision: we have probably never been more aware of our responsibilities towards the environment and other species, but we are persistently irresponsible towards our families and children.

Irresponsible actions damage our relationships with each other and with the world around us. Everyone knows about the devastating consequences of certain actions for the ozone layer, aquatic life or the countryside. The human ecology can also be left in tatters by careless actions, and this is often overlooked.

This is graphically illustrated in our attitudes towards our children and families. John Stuart Mill put it well when he observed that 'the fact itself, of causing the existence of a human being, is one of the most responsible actions in the range of human life'.[1] But do we view the creation of life responsibly? And are we prepared to shoulder the responsibilities which accompany parenthood?

The language of choice and rights

Anyone brought up in the post-1950 period has been fed the language of rights and entitlements with their cornflakes and cod liver oil. The supremacy of individual choice has become the cornerstone of personal decisions and political ideology. All our political parties say the same things about the importance of individual choice – which they are all mindlessly committed to extending. Ironically, they also crave strong family structures and communities which, by definition, can only be created by giving up some of the individualism and rights they regard as inviolable.

An uncivil society

Throughout the past three decades civil society (i.e. our democratic and community institutions) has become *un*civil as modern citizenship has come to be perceived in terms of rights alone. This breeds unrealizable demands, a cult of selfishness. It is bound to flourish in a climate of materialism and consumerism such as we know today, and is further entrenched by individual isolation and by a weakened sense of ethics.

This puts all sorts of new pressures on government and politicians. For example, although the population is now decreasing, we are told we need more than 5 million new homes – creating appalling pressures on the Green Belt and the countryside in general. Why? Because broken families need two homes rather than one.

Rights have replaced duties ... Displaced are the ancient duties to work, to acquire knowledge, to care for the family, to cherish and respect life.

Rights and choices – rather than duty towards family and children – have become our new civic dogma.

Rights have replaced duties as propagandists make demand after demand:

- the right to a job
- the right to an education
- the right to have or to get rid of a child
- the right to take drugs
- the right of access to pornography
- the right to kill
- the right to die

Displaced are our most ancient duties:

- to work
- to acquire knowledge
- to care for the family
- to cherish and respect life

Choices carry consequences

The problem is that choices are no longer conditioned by consequences and the delicate balance of society has been broken. Alisdair MacIntyre powerfully analyses the new conditions in his book *After Virtue*. He says that society has no shared framework for reaching conclusions, because there are so few shared values. People are not encouraged to consider the ethical implications of their actions and communal duty has been abandoned in favour of individual choice. His central question is whether new communal and civic relationships can be snatched from the poisonous clutches of such individualism.[2]

'Choice' is individualism's favourite word and comes from the same Greek root as the word 'heresy'. The modern heresy of choice without consequence is summed up in the murderously loaded phrase 'my right to choose', which could act as a collective epitaph for our times. Me, my, I – these are the words at the heart of the equation: it is not about you or your needs, but mine; it is about rights, not duties; choice, but not the consequences.

This is a fallacy: all choices carry consequences; citizens' rights should be held as a privilege, and there is a return to be made for them. The exercise of individual freedom is invariably at someone else's expense. Freedom for the hunter brings death to the hunted; choice for the rich means starvation for the poor. Yet we are ill prepared for making such choices, for weighing up the consequences. Education has been neutered and, along with parents and the media, simply conditions the people it pretends to teach. Everything, we are told, can be reduced to a matter of personal opinion and everything is relative.

> *The exercise of individual freedom is
> invariably at someone else's expense.*

Right and wrong

Just advocating choice is a poor substitute for preparing for the real and more profound decisions to be made about right and wrong, good and evil. The repetitious mantra of choice is often just a way of dodging the crucial question of consequences.

In the nineteenth century John Stuart Mill argued that unless an action harmed someone else it should be permitted. Out of this has flowed, in the individualistic twentieth century, a catalogue of demands and claimed rights – and a whole new series of concepts about what constitutes 'harm'.

Ethics and shared values have been displaced by individual choice. Worse still, individual choice has been sketched onto the same canvas as the depressing nihilism (i.e. the rejection of all values and beliefs, of all established authority) of Friedrich Nietzsche, the late nineteenth-century German philosopher and so-called 'father of the modern age'. He maintained that the one great freedom was freedom from God, from ultimate accountability. To him, everything that heightened mankind's feeling of power was good; every form of weakness was bad.

A lethal cocktail

At the end of the twentieth century the lethal combination of individualism and Nietzsche's nihilism has left a landscape littered with human casualties – broken-hearted families and broken-backed communities.

> *Fractured families lead to fragmented communities.*

The dehumanization of society and the separation of citizens from their birthright – a sense of belonging, stability and security – have been compounded by the phenomenal growth of mass communications. The family's role as the main transmitter of values, traditions and common culture has been utterly destroyed. That in turn has dangerous implications for liberal democracy and for the very individual liberties which we enjoy. Fractured families lead to fragmented communities. Our parks and streets are no longer safe; women are afraid to go out alone after dark; children cannot be left to play where they want; everyone is vulnerable to muggers or thieves. Individual liberty is curtailed by these dangers: those with no values or respect for others act as they please, while blameless citizens lose out.

If no one is left to transmit a common culture and community values, into what abyss do we fall? The uncontrollability of the mass media seems, if anything, to be accelerating the process of descent.

Discourse by sound-bite

What might, in former times, have been merely the quaint aberration of an obscure group unknown outside its home town spreads rapidly in these multimedia days. Instantaneous communications have robbed us of the ability to think things over, to ponder deeply on serious questions. In public life the sound-bite is all. Considered comment is unwanted, only immediate reactions are welcome. Harm spreads quickly, instantly available to all.

In turn, this has spawned a new ideology: the ideology of virtual reality. Building on the notion that 'if it's right for me, it's right *per se*', the gurus of virtual reality have constructed a world of make-believe where we are encouraged to invent our own values. Ian Mitroff and Warren Bennis argue in *The Unreality Industry* that the deliberate creation of unreality is one of the most important forces shaping contemporary culture. Things unreal, people unreal and behaviour unreal have become a standard point of reference.[3]

Unreal lives

You only have to eavesdrop on conversations at work or on a bus journey to know that people talk endlessly about unreal people in unreal television soaps; that lives are modelled on the flickering lights of a box which has replaced the warmth of the hearth at the centre of our family lives and homes. We have allowed television and the rest of the media to become one of the most potent forces in our personal lives and one of the most powerful influences on our communities and values. A young woman of 16, reflecting ruefully on the dominance of television in her home, and the destruction of family communication, remarked to me, 'I live as a stranger in my own home.'

We have allowed television and the rest of the media to become one of the most potent forces in our personal lives and one of the most powerful influences on our communities and values.

On one occasion in the 1980s, while I was visiting a constituent who had asked me to see her, I had to walk over to a television set and turn it off so that I could actually hear the woman's concerns. Television can be extraordinarily intrusive and encourages a lack of courtesy, be it towards family or visitors.

Television not only destroys conversation but it also defines reality. It blurs the line between fantasy and fact, reality and unreality, truth and lies. Advertising uses this mixture of real and unreal to stimulate a false demand, which in turn leads to unnecessary production and waste. The television hierarchy tells us that there is no correlation between what people watch (unreality) and how they subsequently behave (reality). This would be very convenient if it were not for the advertising industry, who spend a colossal 4 billion pounds annually selling us their wares via television. Presumably they believe this has some effect on those who watch it, otherwise it must constitute a monstrous waste of money.

Man-made God

In our homes virtual reality reinforces a belief in individualism and encourages violence and the rejection of positive values. Through computer software we can kill, maim, brutalize or abuse our victims in 'games' without any apparent consequences. This is the ultimate in personal choice. We start to feel like gods, with all of life's chances and choices at our fingertips. God and creation become nothing but human invention: in virtual reality we make God. For some this is a confirmation of Nietzsche's philosophy that man creates the universe, God is dead and people can become gods. It is a new extension of the serpent's promise in the Garden of Eden.

Broadcasters, film and programme makers and the owners of mass communications have enormous power in forming today's citizens.

- An average adult in Britain spends at least 27 hours a week in front of the television
- Many regularly rent or buy dozens of videos
- Others spend hours surfing the Internet on their personal computers

Occasionally someone from the industry murmurs disapprovingly about the effect of what they are doing. Bruce Gyngell, Managing Director of Tyne Tees Television, asked: 'What are we doing to our sensibilities and moral values and, more important, those of our children, when, day after day, we broadcast an unremitting diet of violence ... television is in danger of becoming a mire of salaciousness and violence.'[4]

A culture of death

One 'high priest' of violence is Oliver Stone. His aptly named film *Natural Born Killers* is surely the apotheosis of all that modern culture holds dear, with its odd mixture of nihilism, liberalism, choice, rights and violence. In this culture of death Stone boasts that 'we' – that is, the manipulators of the mass media – 'poke fun at the idea of righteousness, at the concept that there is a right way and a wrong way'.

Virtual reality not only reinforces nihilism and individualism – it isolates people. In vast numbers of households parents no longer oversee what is viewed by their children, and much of it is unwholesome and destructive.

> *Instead of the wisdom of tradition and*
> *a bequeathed system of values, all we offer*
> *is the right to choose.*

Consumer-driven, materialistic, high-tech, high-powered, information-laden lives are fed by this diet of broken glass. Where will it lead? Instead of the wisdom of tradition and a bequeathed system of values, all we offer is the right to choose. Is that actually worth anything? Where has it left our communities and our families?

Who pays the price?

We have an insatiable fascination with the markets, share prices and the respective values of national currencies. If only we measured political success and failure against the effects on relationships, families and communities rather than what is happening on Wall Street, we would certainly arrive at some radically different conclusions about the health of modern Britain. Materially we are told that we have never been better off, but modern life seems totally unable to meet our hopes and desires. We are told that we are winners, but I have never met so many people who tell me that they are losers.

Who can I blame?

A rights-based culture tends to encourage a 'poor me' response. Everyone regards themselves as victims and the immediate response to every situation is to ask 'Who can I blame? Who can I sue?', or 'What does it matter? Why should I care?' It has been described as a no-blame, no-shame, no-pain society.

Irresponsible attitudes towards our friendships and relationships have left a trail of destruction. This is revealed in the exponential increase in broken families, but also in the way we understand the responsibilities which accompany procreation and parenting.

No more spouses, no more parents

The status of married couples, for example, has been changed dramatically. In 1997, when my wife was expecting our fourth child, the local women's hospital wanted details of her 'partner'. The clerk looked mildly surprised when she said that she had no 'partner'. What is so wrong with husbands having wives and wives having husbands?

A report in October 1997 suggested that Irish Church schools were being encouraged to talk to children about 'adults at home' rather than about 'mammy and daddy'. There is no doubt that many children do not have a father or mother at home, but this further deconstruction of parenthood will do nothing to counter the problem. It merely reinforces it.

Children have been made into commodities.

If the status of parents has been undermined, the status of children has been changed beyond recognition. They have been made into commodities and are treated like possessions which, along with property and accumulated capital, form part of a settlement between a man and woman opting to go their separate ways. People may divorce each other, but they cannot divorce their children. Having taught them to honour and love them as parents, they then divide their children and love often turns to hate. Is it any wonder that children become disorientated and confused?

The rising level of disorder among young people – everything from underachievement at school and juvenile crime to depression, substance abuse and suicide – is hardly coincidence. Even the most hardened liberal apologist can surely see that this is inextricably connected to the breakdown of family life.

Divorce damages children's health

According to research, children are better able to cope with parents fighting and arguing than they are able to cope with a parent leaving. In 1986, Professor Gerald Caplan, Emeritus Professor of Psychiatry at Harvard University, wrote in the *British Medical Journal*: 'There is compelling evidence that divorce exerts a harmful effect on children, over and above the psychological damage that may have been caused by the discord between the parents that led to the separation ... Almost all the children are greatly upset by the break-up of their home.'[5]

When researchers from Exeter University examined children in different family circumstances, the results were striking. Against children from undisturbed homes, those from broken homes were:

- twice as likely to have health or self-worth problems;
- three times as likely to have educational or social problems;
- four times as likely to have behavioural problems.[6]

Professor A.H. Halsey, who has assiduously gathered together research detailing the effects of broken homes on children, arrives at this conclusion: 'On the evidence available, such children tend to die earlier, to have more illness, to do less well at school, to exist at a lower level of nutrition, comfort and conviviality, to suffer more unemployment, to be more prone to deviance and crime, and finally to repeat the cycle of unstable parenting from which they themselves have suffered.'[7] And yet, ad nauseam, we repeat the old excuse that the divorce was 'for the sake of the children'. At best this is self-deception; at worst it is the systematic development of a society in which stable families are eliminated.

Unbreakable bonds

Despite evidence of the type detailed above, many parents continue to persuade themselves that they are breaking their promises, ripping up their marriage covenants, in the best interests of the children. In fact, the children are often pushed like pawns from one square to the next as their parents play games at their expense. It is bogus to pretend that a separation is crucial to the child's interests if the only thing the adults are interested in is their own personal happiness. From seeing every divorce as a tragedy, it is now viewed by many as an insurance policy for personal satisfaction.

Allan Bloom, in *The Closing of the American Mind*, puts it starkly enough: 'Of course many families are unhappy. But that is irrelevant. The important lesson that the family teaches is the existence of the only unbreakable bond, for better or for worse, between human beings.'[8] Bloom implies that families can come through their unhappiness, but lawyers whose salaries are earned by deconstructing marriages are rarely interested in achieving that. There was unhappiness in marriages in earlier generations, but they tended to stick at it and try again – on for the sake of their children. Even before they begin today there is an expectation in the minds of many couples that there will be other weddings and other partners. For children it is an unmitigated disaster.

A powerful indictment

In one primary school in my own north-west region of England, of the 170 families with children at the school just six had a father at home. Whole streets and neighbourhoods are without worthwhile male role models and this has a woeful effect on the children.

Many children have effectively had their childhood taken away.

While working for several years with children who had special needs, I met young people who were seriously underachieving because of the traumatic circumstances of their broken homes. Sadly they were not rarities. The *Sunday Times* columnist Melanie Phillips in *All Must Have Prizes*, her admirable account of how parents and schools have failed our young people, says that traumatized family life helps to explain why 10,000 children were excluded from schools in 1995, some as young as four years old. She quotes a Doncaster head teacher who said that many children 'have effectively had their childhood taken away'.

In a powerful indictment Melanie Phillips writes: 'Having a child thus changed from being the fulfilment of a covenant with the future to being the completion of an adult's egotistic ambitions … The outcome is children who are rootless, unhappy and often out of control.'[9]

False liberalism

Through legislation like the 1989 Children Act, we tell children that they, too, have any number of rights – but we seem oblivious to their deeper needs and dependence on adults, and to our duties towards those children. The 1989 legislation was a response to the abuse of children in institutional care, but instead of offering them better protection we offered another batch of rights. Has it worked? Apparently not.

- There are currently 120,000 registered paedophiles in the UK.
- There are 46,000 children on child protection registers at risk of physical or sexual abuse.
- Abuse of children continues unabated – often with the connivance of people in authority.

We are forever treating symptoms with the wrong medicines and ignoring the cause of the malady. Whatever their rights, children are at risk from many dangers, and we are not fulfilling our duty of care.

Whether at home or in school, it is cruel and misguided to abandon children to *laissez-faire* teaching methods, to myriad legal provisions, or to a false liberalism which pretends that rules do not matter, offering choices instead of love and the guiding hand of parental authority.

Children are at risk from many dangers
and we are not fulfilling our duty of care.

Abandoning parental responsibility and, for instance, allowing children to watch what they want for as long as they want on television, or letting them try out whatever they want (be it drink, drugs, or crime), is a recipe for social chaos. Children are simply not equipped to make up their own minds about complex issues which adults find challenging enough. False liberalism pretends that by not disapproving or correcting we are somehow being tolerant. Children are entitled to view this sort of parental response as mere indifference. Guidance is a necessary part of the learning process until young people can measure up relative values and decide for themselves from a position of knowledge.

Any brand on the shelf

Children should not be conned into believing that every view or opinion is of equal worth. Presumably a historian would not accept that a revisionist view of the Holocaust, denying the enormity of the carnage, was of equal worth with a truthful account; or that from the perspective of the debris of Soviet society we have to accept the validity of Marxist ideology. All views are not of equal worth.

The Dalai Lama has wisely reminded western educationalists that before children are taught about Buddhism they need to understand their own Christian religion properly. As adults we can embrace or reject what we have been taught – and we are better equipped to make comparisons – but simplistic syncretism is no preparation for five- or ten-year-olds. They end up understanding nothing and rejecting everything.

We should not feel constrained to support a false liberalism that treats all brands on the shelf as the same. This false liberalism has bequeathed us a society in which we are encouraged to believe that self-gratification is paramount: if it feels good, do it. How does this work out in our attitude towards our children?

Everything once had a value; now it has a price.

What's in it for me?

A 1990 Eurobarometer survey of European attitudes towards the family was deeply revealing.[10] The survey found that in Portugal 68 per cent, in Greece 63 per cent and in Spain 58 per cent of those who took part believed that the most important role of the family was bringing up and educating the children. In the United Kingdom the figure was just 24 per cent – most British respondents believed that families were about personal adult fulfilment. Everything in Britain is measured in terms of 'what's in it for me?'. Everything once had a value; now it has a price.

Sneering contempt

False liberalism has encouraged a sneering contempt for the traditional, stable family unit while it apparently venerates any other configuration of living arrangements. This is an appalling mistake. In the Introduction I mentioned that Francis Fukuyama points to 1967 as 'the year of the great disruption'.

This was the year when a crime became an act of medical compassion, when the Hippocratic Oath was discarded, and when the inalienable right to life was subjected to the question of choice. It was also the year in which the anthropologist Edmund Leach gave his now notorious judgement on the family: 'Far from being the basis of a good society, the family, with its narrow privacy and tawdry secrets, is the source of all our discontents.'[11]

Leach's caricature of the family as the enemy of personal happiness epitomizes the spirit of false liberalism. There is no doubt that some families were and are unhappy. Some family situations may suffocate or trap, but Henry David Thoreau was right when he said that if you cut down all the trees there will be nowhere left for the birds to sing. Cutting down the family may have served a false liberal theory, but it has left no safe place for children to be nurtured and for people to realize their full potential.

The extended family

I am not a particular advocate of what many describe as 'the nuclear family'. For me it smacks too much of a perfectly synchronized, regimented approach and bears little resemblance to the untidy, extended families which have historically transmitted values, provided a network of care and dealt together with the misfortunes of life. For those who feel comfortable with concepts of community, it would be absurd to exclude the most important and foundational community of all.

Untidy, extended families have historically transmitted values, provided a network of care and dealt together with the misfortunes of life.

I was first struck by the enduring strength of the extended family 25 years ago, as a young City Councillor representing a tough and economically deprived corner of inner-city Liverpool. Children born outside wedlock were frequently brought up alongside other children and grandchilden. Grandparents, aunts and uncles, fathers and mothers, all shared each other's burdens and responsibilities.

I was also struck by the 'we-know-best' elitism promoted by the liberal intelligentsia who populated planning offices and Council politics rather than the back streets of the city. They wantonly destroyed self-sufficient communities and wreaked havoc with their bulldozing, redevelopment and social engineering. The greatest casualty was the extended family, as young people were marooned on faceless, sprawling sink estates, devoid of both amenities and humanity, splitting families apart. These municipal ghettos have bred a generation of young people who have been reared without the close support systems of the extended family. The ever-present social workers and probation officers have been poor substitutes for fathers, grandparents, aunts and uncles.

Not just the children

The other consequence of these calamitous policies has been the isolation of elderly relatives, often left in the inner city without kith and kin nearby. In Liverpool the fastest-growing section of the population are the over-eighties, and one in four citizens is over retirement age. By contrast, the overspill estates of Kirkby, where I taught in the early 1970s, reputedly had the largest number of children per head of population anywhere in Western Europe. Planning policies, exacerbated by all the other trends which I have described, militated against the continued flourishing of the delicate mutual support system of the extended family.

I am reminded of the story of a young Nigerian woman who trained in geriatric medicine and who came to Liverpool to undertake a further course. She did not bother completing it, but returned to West Africa because, as she pointedly remarked, 'you have nothing to teach us about the care of the elderly'. The contrast between how we treat our elderly relatives and how they are cared for in developing nations could not be greater. What has happened to our duty of care to both the youngest and the oldest in our community? In Britain the Cambridge-based Jubilee Centre estimates that a million elderly people do not see either a friend, a relative or a neighbour during the course of an average week.

In the early 1990s, Mother Teresa of Calcutta, speaking at the White House, told of a recent visit she had made to a home for old people. She had noticed how the surroundings were materially very affluent. Why then, she had asked her companion, are they all staring at the door? Because they are waiting for relatives who never come, was the reply.

The least worst alternative

Winston Churchill once famously remarked that democracy is the least worst form of government. The family may also be far from perfect, but it is proven to be the best instrument available for promoting stability and security, for providing educational support and for developing the personal responsibility and sense of duty needed to ensure social harmony. Worse alternatives are all around us today. If responsible citizens do not fight to protect family life, the consequences will be dire.

The family may be far from perfect,
but it is proven to be the best instrument
available for promoting stability and security.

What can we do?

In the past 10 years 1.6 million children in Britain have been affected by their parents' divorce. If we want to see this figure reduced we can, at a personal level, renew our vows and promise our children that we will stick by them. We can organize our lives to ensure that we have more time for our families and children. At the level of political decision-making we can insist that candidates and their parties outline the ways in which they intend to take pressure off families.

Some hold that family life has little to do with politicians. This is not so. Politicians are closely involved with issues which have a direct bearing on families and children, such as divorce, employment, welfare, education, abortion and adoption. Law-makers enact legislation which can make it easier or harder for marriages to break up; they determine fiscal priorities which can either encourage or discriminate against the family.

New priorities

When British Telecom launched one of its biggest and most expensive television advertising campaigns – 'Why can't daddy get home for bath time?' – it followed a theme explored by Rob Parsons in his highly readable *Sixty Minute Father*, which examined the amount of time fathers spend with their children.[12]

In the BT advertisement a nine-year-old schoolgirl, Nicola, travels to her father's office to see what keeps him there until after 8.00 p.m. most evenings. Nicola's father is one of the many who spend more time day-dreaming or drinking tea at the office than in discussion or activity with their children. He is also likely to spend considerably longer each day watching television than doing anything with his children – so perhaps the medium of a television advertisement was rather a good way of challenging fathers to reorder their priorities.

Further evidence of distorted priorities appeared when the *Daily Telegraph* reported the findings of a survey which they had commissioned in 1997. It found that some parents deliberately work additional hours as a way of escaping the strains of family life.

Working patterns

BT commissioned some research and a report based on their advertisement. They claim that on average just three minutes of 'quality time' is spent by fathers with their children each day. BT conclude that if we used more of the information technologies which they sell, we could save wasted time at work (which they estimate costs the UK £47 million annually) and use this time for our families instead.

---

*On average just three minutes of 'quality time'
is spent by fathers with their children each day.*

If social workers had carried out the survey, doubtless they would have told us that the answer would be found in the appointment of more social workers. Would it not be better to reorder our priorities? We have never worked longer hours. The elimination by Parliament of Sunday as a special day for rest and recreation is only the latest example of the erosion of family time. Ridiculously long hours are spent at work.

- One in five managers and directors are at work by 7.30 a.m.
- One in three regularly work later than 8.00 p.m.
- Seven in ten regularly work at weekends or on bank holidays.

Nowadays many women work away from the home and, often despite themselves, families become trapped by financial commitments which rely on two incomes. Millions of children have increasingly fewer encounters with their parents and more and more are left with child-minders. We must find a way to escape from this treadmill, and challenge the creation of conditions in which we become economic slaves, with husbands and wives both forced into the jobs market in order to sustain high mortgages and a whole range of other commitments.

During the summer of 1997 the high-flying, highly paid President of the Pepsi Cola Corporation, Brenda Barnes, announced that she was quitting her $1.24 million p.a. job to spend time with her baby, from whom she felt increasingly estranged. She had her priorities right, but then again she had the resources to make such a decision possible. Every couple should be given the same opportunity. Instead, the 1998 European Working Time Directive could lead to some employees working for 12 days at a time, without a day off.

Politicians must understand the economic and social costs of leaving children in the hands of strangers, isolated from their parents, and reorder our employment laws and our tax and benefit system accordingly. At present the burden of taxation falls disproportionately on one-earner married couples with families. Flexible work-patterns and employment legislation which supports the family – and an equivalent income equal to any minimum wage for those mothers who choose to work at home with their children – might be part of this package of reforms.

Parents not minders

Ominously, however, the first Budget of the New Labour Government did not augur well for the family.

- £200 million spent on getting lone mothers 'back' to work (are they not working now?)
- Some of the £200 million to go towards training 50,000 child-care workers (are child-minders an improvement on mothers?)
- Married couples' allowance kept at a pitiful £200 a year

The next Budget made matters worse, reducing the married couples' allowance even further and provoking the charge that it was a £720 million tax on marriage and motherhood. Twenty years ago a married couple with one working spouse on average earnings, with a mortgage and two children, paid 12 per cent of their income in tax and national insurance. Today they contribute more than 20 per cent.

Propagandists, especially those who oppose traditional ideas of parenting, claim that 90 per cent of all lone mothers want to work away from the home. In fact, the surveys which suggest these percentages also reveal that two out of ten want to work '*at some point in the future*' but only three out of ten want to work while their children are small. If lone mothers do go away from home to work, the child is left without any full-time parent to care for them.

If both parents are out at work, who will bring up the children? Increasing numbers of children are being dumped for long hours with anonymous child-carers. Homework clubs and after-school care merely add to the State's feeble attempts to provide a life-support system for the family. They will never be a substitute for a parent at home and they will consolidate the makeshift arrangements that give children dangerously precarious lives. This has got to be the wrong priority.

If both parents are out at work,
who will bring up the children?

Better priorities would surely recognize these three vital points:

- Children have need of two committed parents, one at home with them full-time when they are very young.
- When one parent opts to stay at home to care for a child, this is the most loving sacrifice a person can make.
- The tax and benefit system, along with employment law, should allow people the economic freedom to be full-time mothers – or full-time fathers, for that matter.

Women who have raised families have a crucial contribution to make to the economy. But the decision about when and if they should return to work outside the home must rest entirely with them – and the Government could usefully assist this process by providing for more retraining, and for more part-time and term-time working opportunities.

Attack poverty not parents

Children are not the only ones to miss out through wrong-headed priorities. Family poverty is not alleviated by forcing both parents into work. Low-income families will simply end up struggling to pay increasing child-care bills. If the Chancellor allowed a non-earning wife or husband to transfer their unused tax allowance to the earner, it would be a more worthwhile contribution to strengthening family life than training up armies of child-care workers. Those in power should spend more time attacking poverty and less time undermining parents. We need equitable and honest taxation. Reducing taxes for some does not equate with addressing injustice and inequality.

Those in power should spend more time attacking poverty and less time undermining parents.

Who's pulling your strings?

Why should we accept the assumption that what children want and need is a working mother? Why should we accept that it is best if both parents go out to work? Why should we accept the anonymous and soulless arrangements for child-care which the State is dreaming up? Who is making our priorities, pulling our strings?

A State that wanted to send the right signals about the importance of the family would use financial incentives to encourage and reward families who stay together. During the passage of the 1996 Family Law Bill I argued for Anniversary Tax Allowances – tax breaks which might be given incrementally as wedding anniversaries occur. I also suggested that Family Impact Statements should be attached to every new Government policy, just as local authorities attach environmental impact statements to planning applications and policies. At least then politicians would have to evaluate the effect their proposals would have on the family, ensuring, for the first time, that this issue becomes a central political concern.

Individual citizens can take action to force politicians to see family policy as a central issue. It is a question to raise at every opportunity with election candidates and MPs, with political parties and with the Government. At a personal level we can also decide to weigh up more carefully whether we are prepared to accept the duties and responsibilities which married life and parenting brings.

End divorce on demand

The State should also re-evaluate the 'divorce-on-demand' laws and the foolish decision to abolish the concept of fault. I was one of a handful of MPs who voted against the third reading of the Family Law Act. I did so because Parliament was living in an unreal world by pretending that statute could wish away fault. Ever since Henry VIII began his assault on marriage and the family – and institutionalized promise-breaking – successive government interventions have made the position worse.

Self-sacrifice and mutual support

Within all our homes we must transmit to our children the experience and knowledge accumulated over centuries that generosity, forgiveness, self-sacrifice and mutual support are a crucial part of family life, and vital for the survival of the wider community. Parents can either let their children wander into the cul-de-sac of selfishness, or they can lead them by example onto the open road of love.

Generosity, forgiveness, self-sacrifice and
mutual support are a crucial part of family life,
and vital for the survival of the wider community.

It is an illusion to maintain that life brings no pain, no set-backs, no disappointments, no faults. But life's troubles are easier to face in community, with the support and strength of a complete family for security.

In earlier generations many husbands and wives weathered the storms and survived incidents which today are resolved by an immediate call to the lawyer and a subsequent divorce. We need to develop a greater resolve to work things through and to carry on despite mistakes. Parents are often derided as 'dishonest' for staying together 'for the sake of the children' when their own relationship seems to have broken down, but that seems a perfectly good reason to me, given the determination to see it through. I have a friend whose marriage ran into serious trouble about 10 years ago. The couple resolved to see their youngest child into university before they split up. By the time this happened, their earlier differences had long since been smoothed out and they remain happily married today.

Children at heart

In reordering our political and personal priorities, we must insist on a shift back to the *child's* welfare and needs as the foremost consideration. Our policies and individual actions must revolve around our children – creating stability and security for their proper development. The interests of the adults must come second. The implications for personal and public policy on a range of issues from abortion to adoption, from fiscal policies to divorce, are glaringly obvious. The responsible parent, the responsible citizen, will want to radically reassess their whole approach to these questions.

Essential Questions

- Which would you put first: your individual rights or duty to your family?
- Who and what are your priorities?
- Are economic demands destroying the time you can spend with your family?
- Do you allow videos, the Internet or television to dominate your family life?
- Would you question or challenge friends or relatives who say they are seeking a divorce?
- Have you ever asked a politician about his or her policies towards the extended family? Is there a way you could do that in your local constituency?
- Do you have a considered political view about how family and community life might best be strengthened?

2/ Citizen Values

John Ruskin once wrote that 'A nation cannot last as a money-making mob; it cannot, with impunity, go on despising literature, despising science, despising art, despising nature, despising compassion.'[1] And yet the 1990s, certainly until the summer of 1997, will largely be remembered as a time of grasping individualism where enough was always a little bit more, and where the rules were largely drawn up by the money-making mob. Of course, money is crucial to the management of our personal and communal affairs, but the way it is used need not be left entirely in the hands of fast-talking city-types and greedy corporations. A growing understanding that investment in the markets can bring opportunities for positive influence, as well as financial returns, is tempering the worst excesses of the 'mob'. It also gives the individual citizen a vital chance to put his or her values and ethics into action.

The difference we can make

The 1990s have seen a developing awareness that the actions of individuals can shape events and alter priorities.

My early experience of the effectiveness of personal direct action was as a teenage schoolboy. War in Biafra had brought shocking pictures of children dying of starvation. I organized a sponsored all-night walk round our school playing fields and was amazed by the generous response of those who took part and those who gave money.

At university my first speech to the Student Union was in support of the campaign to Stop The Seventies Tour – of South Africa's racially selected rugby team. With a friend, I subsequently managed to gain admittance to a press conference organized by a South African trade delegation. We embarrassed them with some awkward questions about apartheid. Many of us also boycotted Barclays Bank because of their support at the time for apartheid-ridden institutions.

As a young City Councillor – and later as Liverpool's Housing Chairman – I was directly able to affect policies which determined the housing conditions of thousands of people, as well as issues such as the purchasing policy of the Local Authority's Central Purchasing Unit, or its planning and land use priorities.

In Parliament the establishment of the Jubilee Campaign – to champion the human rights of people suffering because of their religious beliefs – meant that dozens of individual cases in numerous countries were highlighted and successfully resolved.

---

*Whatever the issue at stake, each of us
can make a difference.*

All these activities proved to me the effect which an individual can have on an institution or government. Whatever the issue at stake, each of us can make a difference. These days, one of the most important areas where individuals can campaign to uphold values is the financial arena, both in terms of consumer action and investment.

Consumer clout

This growing awareness of how our individual actions can affect others for good or ill is especially relevant in a consumerist age where the language of choice is such common currency. If we choose to buy this product rather than another, or to invest in this company or investment fund rather than another, we directly affect a vast range of individuals and institutions. Information is now widely available on how to invest ethically. If we are really concerned about upholding values in this arena, we should appreciate the power of money and learn how to use that power to affect company policies. Companies are increasingly aware that the consumer can withdraw support for a product with devastating results.

Voting with their cash

During the 1980s I tabled parliamentary motions and questions in the Commons concerning food which had been irradiated. The big vested interests involved with these products vowed they were safe, but such was their confidence in the public's unquestioning acceptance of irradiated products that they had not specifically labelled them. Consumers protested; the Government issued a requirement that irradiated goods should be labelled. Shoppers voted with their feet – and their cash – and walked past the shelves of irradated products. They were withdrawn.

Today our supermarkets are full of genetically manipulated foods – many involving the mixing of animal and human genes. When, or if, a similar requirement is made for all genetically modified products to be labelled, we may see a similarly strong response of consumer rejection for the tampered goods.

Companies are increasingly aware that the consumer can withdraw support for a product with devastating results.

Anyone seriously wishing to find out more about particular consumer issues can turn to publications such as *The Ethical Consumer* magazine for in-depth information.

Going bananas over ethics

Bananas, to take one example, have been much in the news in recent years. A familiar and harmless sight in everyone's fruit-bowl, of course, but also the focus of a widespread ethical campaign. Consumers are playing a vital ongoing role in the drive to force banana companies to improve their practices. The World Development Movement (WDM) has been asking customers to put pressure on Del Monte, Chiquita and Dole – three multinationals who control two-thirds of the world banana trade. In Britain the banana is our most popular fruit, but what these major companies do to get the banana onto our tables is pretty shocking.

- All three companies pressurize their workers to forgo legitimate union rights.
- They fail to meet acceptable health standards.

- Banana workers in countries like Costa Rica have been left sterile or suffering chronic ill health because of the excessive use of sprays and pesticides (also, of course, detrimental to the environment and possibly the consumers of the fruit).
- Long hours and unsafe conditions are the staple fare of many.

WDM tell the stories of Maria and Pedro as examples. Maria's baby son was born with a head four times bigger than his body. His mouth and nose were joined together. His mother said: 'I couldn't even hold him because it made things worse, so I just talked to him and cried with him.'

Maria's husband Juan worked on a Costa Rican banana plantation and used the pesticide DBCP, which has been linked with sterility and other health problems. DBCP has now been banned, but other toxic chemicals have not. Leaving aside the irreversible destruction of primary tropical forest, over-intensive cultivation of bananas has made the crop more susceptible to black sigatoka fungus – and the banana companies respond by spraying toxic fungicides from the air. Wildlife, aquatic life, biodiversity and plantation workers and their families are all harmed as a consequence.

It's the profit which makes things so expensive.

Pedro's employers, Chiquita, cut his wages by a staggering 70 per cent and forced him to leave his union. According to WDM, workers on Del Monte plantations say it is dangerous even to mention the word 'union'. *The Ethical Consumer* quoted Doris Calvo, a Costa Rican banana packer sacked for her union activities, as saying: 'Behind this fruit, which tastes so sweet, are the tears and deaths of human beings. It is the lives of our workers which are being sold over there.'[2]

The average Latin American plantation worker receives just 1–2 per cent of what consumers pay for the fruit. It's the profit which makes things so expensive.

The best of the bunch

WDM has been organizing a campaign whereby customers are urged to write to these companies telling them they want to be able to buy bananas grown in safe working conditions. (They are not calling yet for an all-out boycott on buying the bananas, as this could cost the workers their livelihood.) It is a good example of how the individual consumer can act ethically.

Christian Aid's 'Global Supermarket' campaign takes the issue further and seeks supermarket commitment to corporate codes of conduct, including respect for basic labour rights. Such pressure has already led to all the major banana companies producing their first drafts of such codes. Of course, without independent monitoring (the companies have promised to monitor themselves), the codes become worthless pieces of paper – only of propaganda value to the banana companies. But at least it is one step in the right direction.

Consumers can also be discriminating in what they buy. The labelling of bananas produced in equitable circumstances as 'Fair Trade Bananas' is on the way and, meanwhile, campaigners have advised consumers to 'Buy Windward Islands, the best of the bunch' (labelled St Vincent, Dominica, St Lucia, Grenada, Martinique and 5 Isles).

Knowledge is power

Whatever the product, establishing a country of origin and knowing something about the practices of those countries is crucial for the citizen looking to buy ethically. The Catholic Aid Agency (CAFOD), for example, looked into the manufacture of shoes in developing countries:

- Workers are routinely exposed to dangerous glues and solvents.
- They are forced to work long hours for little reward.
- In Brazil children are frequently exposed to toxic fumes while working near glue pots, suffering from neurological damage, breathing difficulties and stunted growth as a result.
- In China, rates of pay were found to be as low as 12p an hour – with typical shifts of 13 hours, seven days a week.

Faced with such facts, what can we do to bring pressure to bear on the perpetrators? At the very least, we can choose to buy different shoes (or whatever the product is) so that we as individuals are not supporting a company which forces its workers to suffer such appalling conditions.

Citizens can opt to spend their money more ethically.

Sustaining the planet

Using recycled goods is another example of how citizens can opt to spend their money more ethically – and make a contribution to sustainability. Recycled paper, for instance, brings the following benefits during manufacture compared to the production of ordinary paper:

- Reduction of water consumption by nearly 60 per cent
- Reduction in energy consumption by 40 per cent
- Reduction in air pollution by 74 per cent
- Reduction in water pollution by 35 per cent

Five million tons of paper are still landfilled every year in the UK – creating greenhouse gases 25 per cent more dangerous than carbon dioxide. According to the Paper Federation's Annual Review, this waste also has an economic impact: in addition to the environmental costs, there is also a loss to the economy. UK national income actually rises by £154 for every ton of paper which is recycled.

The ethical citizen will want to see all goods clearly labelled, recording the relevant data about recycled components and environmental concerns. We need to campaign for the freedom to make informed choices about everything we buy.

Company agendas

Companies such as Body Shop have developed a whole agenda around a more ethical approach:

- A clear rejection of animal testing for cosmetics (a principle now followed by a number of other companies)

- Charitable giving (nearly 3 per cent of pre-tax profits compared with a UK company average of 0.26 per cent)
- Environmental awareness
- Commitment to Trade Not Aid producers (in reality still less than 1 per cent of worldwide sales)
- The use wherever possible of 'natural' rather than synthetic ingredients

Sometimes a small shareholding in companies less enlightened than Body Shop can shame them into changing their policies. Possessing shares gives you more clout if you write to the company managers about a particular issue. You may also gain access to annual meetings of shareholders, where you can table resolutions or speak against specific investment policies or unethical practices conducted by the company.

Every effort against a bad policy makes a difference.

In 1995, Friends of the Earth took on the mining giants RTZ over the issue of environmental values. At the company's Annual General Meeting their Chief Executive, Robert Wilson, was made to admit that a mining project in Madagascar could lead to the extinction of two species and to the loss of 50 per cent of Madagascar's remaining coastal forest. Although the meeting was unconvinced by Friends of the Earth's argument, RTZ was forced to detail its activities publicly – always the first step in achieving a change of policy.

Every effort against a bad policy makes a difference. Sometimes pressure has to be maintained for some time before that difference is achieved, but it is essential not to lose heart and to keep challenging where important ethical issues are at stake.

In February 1998, for example, I visited refugee camps on the Burma–Thailand border. Through the Jubilee Campaign, which I helped to found, we are running a disinvestment and non-purchasing campaign directed at the British company Premier Oil and the French company Total. Despite the decision of the American Congress to ban new investment in Burma because of monstrous human rights abuses (an estimated 20,000 dead in the past five years), Premier and Total are still pursuing lucrative oil deals with the Burmese military government. As Archbishop Desmond Tutu has pointed out, in the context of South Africa, the weapon which finally destroyed apartheid was economic disinvestment. From their offices at St John's, Wonersh, in Guildford, Jubilee has organized information packs and protest cards which can be sent direct to the two companies and to the Foreign Secretary, Robin Cook, urging them to follow the lead of the American Congress, and thus bring pressure to bear on the Burmese government to improve its human rights record.

The weapon which finally destroyed apartheid was economic disinvestment.

Piecemeal and individual responses certainly have their place, but we all know that even the Government's actions are often restricted by the powerful global influence of multinational companies and the investment funds on which they and the markets rely. What opportunities are there here for the citizen who wants to be ethical? Is there any way to influence these global corporations and investment funds? The answer is yes, if enough 'small stones' act together.

Going ethical

Robin Cook's declared intention of creating 'an ethical foreign policy' is a good example of the increasing and widespread belief that politics and commerce should maintain high ethical standards. Blatant excesses – from the House of Commons 'cash for questions' affair to City of London scams and scandals – have created a climate in which there seems to be a general desire by companies and institutions to 'go ethical'.

While some may announce that they have 'gone ethical' for purely cosmetic reasons, many companies and individuals are sincerely motivated and some have already experienced a fundamental conversion. A range of organizations – including the Ethical Investment Research Service (EIRIS) and the UK Social Investment Forum – through their 'Tomorrow's Company' campaign, have

helped create this sea change. More and more companies and institutions are considering their responsibility to all their stakeholders:
the wider community, employees and individual shareholders alike.

There is still what the Industrial Society has described as an 'ethics
gap' between the rhetoric and the reality, however. In a recent
survey of 300 business managers, the Society said that while more
than half believed in an ethical approach, just 30 per cent said that
this was actually what their companies did.

Good ethics does not mean bad business.
The reverse is true.

In his book *The Ethical Investor* Russell Sparkes drew on his day-to-
day experience as Secretary to the Methodist Church's Joint Advisory
Committee on the Ethics of Investment to argue cogently for ethical
priorities and to demolish the myth that investing ethically is
incompatible with good business returns. Sparkes said the social
economy is 'a form of economic organisation not centred around
money, but on a sense of shared values' such as co-operatives.[3]

Good ethics does *not* mean bad business. The reverse is true:

- The ethical trust sector has experienced a 34 per cent
  growth since 1989.
- This is double the 17 per cent average growth of all unit and
  investment trusts over the same period.

This success has certainly contributed to the changing perceptions of
those willing to reconsider their business values.

Ethical trusts

In November 1997 Alan Burton, the Chief Executive of Standard
Life, said: 'There has been a general change in public sentiment and
independent financial advisers are telling us that an ethical fund will
appeal to a wider section of the market.' He announced that
Standard Life was considering the establishment of an ethical unit
trust (i.e. a trust which screens out investments in companies in-

volved in the arms trade or environmental exploitation, for instance) as part of its range, and confirmed that a changing popular attitude had forced brokers to answer more questions about a company's ethical outlook. There are other signs of promise, too:

- A Friends Provident survey suggests that up to 85 per cent of advisers now recommend ethical funds.
- EIRIS have doubled the number of independent financial advisers they recommend.
- £1.6 billion is now invested in 34 UK ethical funds, 12 of which are unit trust.

Trusts with an ethical edge continue to attract growing sums of investors' money and, if once they were perceived as a do-gooder nutty fringe, that is definitely no longer the case.

Pension funds will surely follow the trail blazed over the past 15 years by unit and investment trusts. The Government, too, has woken up to the possibilities, with the Department for International Development exploring ways in which public–private partnerships can focus on ethical trade and investment.

Investment in ethics

EIRIS has a definition of 'ethical' in an investment context as taking into consideration non-financial factors, including:

- the environment;
- working conditions;
- animal testing.

Before deciding on an investment opportunity, individual consumers might want to add to this list by considering the following aspects too:

- health (e.g. tobacco);
- bioethics (e.g. human embryo experimentation and some form of genetic engineering);
- violence (e.g. arms sales);
- exploitation (e.g. attitudes towards developing countries).

The key in all these questions is to obtain detailed knowledge of an institution's investments and policies, and to know how to exert pressure and who to target.

Using share power

Fund managers have great clout. In 1996, Carol Galley, the chairwoman of Mercury Asset Management (MAM), ensured that the fund manager played a crucial role as a shareholder when Granada launched its hostile takeover bid of Forte. With a 15 per cent stake in both Forte and Granada, MAM swung behind Granada's £3.8 billion bid, enabling it to succeed.

Ethical shareholders can use their right to cast votes and insist that ethical questions are placed on the agenda.

A whole host of fund managers and 'ethically challenged' companies (i.e. those who have opted to pursue high ethical standards) could play an equally pivotal role in shaping company policies. Concerned shareholders can use their right to cast votes and insist that ethical questions are placed on the agenda. In turn, many investors will feel drawn – especially in a more compassionate and aware society – to those funds which can demonstrate a keen sense of ethics or community involvement.

It is an insult to investors to imply that the only factor which motivates them is greed. Certainly, many would not wish to perceive themselves in that way. Most people would prefer to do some good than otherwise. If being good were easy, more people would do it: a company with an ethical approach makes it easier for its investors to do some good in a reasonably painless way. Similarly, companies these days are generally keen to avoid bruising public confrontations, or the bad public relations of being perceived as dirty neighbours or environmentally irresponsible, for example. Having a clear ethical policy makes it easier for them to behave better. The ethical impulse cuts both ways and everyone benefits.

Ethical business boom

Among the leading lights in promoting a code of ethical investment has been Friends Provident. At the persistent urging of Charles Jacob, the then Investment Manager of the Central Finance Board of the Methodist Church (CFB), they launched the first ethical unit trust. For ten years, from 1973, Jacob battled to persuade an unwilling Department of Trade to allow a unit trust 'to combine capital and conscience'.[4] After its launch, Stewardship funds doubled in three years to break through the £800 million barrier.

At long last we are seeing the integration
of ethics and economics.

Friends Provident's assistant product manager, Phil White, told *Financial Adviser*: 'At its launch, sceptics dismissed Stewardship as a fad or gimmick and said it wouldn't last, but 13 years of decent returns have proved them wrong.'[5] The Stewardship Trust has a distinctive and proactive ethical basis as its appeal. Not content with simply *screening out* companies involved in dubious practices – which was the extent of 'ethical' action in the 1980s – the new approach is to *search out* companies which exhibit a strong sense of social responsibility, as well as to probe their negative practices (i.e. what they are doing *and* not doing), before committing to investments.

Companies with an ethical edge could be boom businesses in the future as clients appreciate that their ability to make good returns on their investments need not be adversely affected by taking a strong ethical position. At long last we are seeing the integration of ethics and economics.

Pension power

About two-thirds of the stock market is owned by insurance companies and pension funds. Although this is our money, 'we the people' have very little practical influence over how it is used. Most people will say they have no stocks or shares, but in reality their pensions and insurance cover are invested on their behalf in any number of stocks and shares.

Eighteen million people in Britain have an occupational or personal pension plan. EIRIS have published further evidence confirming the public's wish to be ethical citizens in financial terms. They conducted a poll through NOP in September 1997, questioning participants about pension funds which operate an ethical policy.

- 73 per cent said yes to ethical pensions.
- Over 44 per cent said their pension scheme should operate an ethical policy – if it could be done without reduction in the financial return.
- 29 per cent were prepared to see a reduction in their return.
- Women were twice as willing as men to forgo profit for ethics.
- The most favoured investments were in companies with a good record on the environment, customer care and employment conditions.
- The least favoured companies were those manufacturing weapons, undertaking testing on animals, breaking 'green' regulations and investing in countries with oppressive regimes.

Taking the initiative

The last point in the list above raises the question, 'What *is* ethical?' Where is the line drawn? How much information should be available? For instance, it should be made clear what ethical criteria are being used in the screening-out process. Until recently, no company was screened out for involvement in genetics, cloning, eugenics, abortion, euthanasia or embryo experimentation. Recognizing this ethical gap, the Banner Group, of which I am a non-executive director, has been exploring ways of addressing the problem.

In the summer of 1998 Banner launched their Real Life Investment Portfolio. They have 4,000 clients worldwide and invited the company Albert E. Sharp (AES) to become the fund manager. AES has £5 billion of funds under management, including ethical funds worth £250 million. Banner Director Howard Tingley says, 'Many ethical investment funds focus on the environment, the planet, etc., and whilst these aims are commendable we believe the focus should be on the sanctity of human life.'

Real Life Investments are made in companies which:

- provide positive support for employees during pregnancy and make generous provision for paternity and maternity leave;
- make special provision for disabled employees and generally provide a high standard of employee welfare;
- supply the necessities of life;
- strive to avoid handling goods produced by exploited labour forces overseas;
- act to conserve energy and natural resources, to reduce waste and control pollution;
- publicly profess their commitment to pro-life values.

Real Life also operate negative investment criteria, refusing to invest in companies which:

- manufacture, sell, distribute or in any way promote the sale of abortion equipment, or abortion-linked pharmaceuticals, including RU486 and the 'morning-after pill';
- support or subsidize destructive human embryo research or ethically questionable genetic engineering;
- are involved in the provision of pharmaceuticals for or research into euthanasia;
- support oppressive regimes or companies which exploit labour in the developing world, or whose products are detrimental to the general population in countries with a poor human rights record;
- perform tests on animals for purposes other than the advancement of human health;
- have a poor environmental record;
- are involved in pornography;
- participate in the sale of arms, tobacco, or alcohol;
- who derive more than 3 per cent of their income from gambling.

Banner's Real Life approach to ethical investment is a brave and exciting initiative. It extends the debate about 'what is ethical'. This debate will be broadened further as people begin to see that the choices they make about pension investments can also be used to affect company ethics.

There is colossal public support for
an ethical approach to pension funds.

Although there is colossal public support for an ethical approach, the only people who can currently *choose* to have a pension with such a policy are people with personal pension plans. How many occupational schemes provide for this clearly expressed ethical preference? The Pensions Act does require funds to provide a statement of their investment principles, though ethical issues need not be specifically mentioned. The Goode Committee Report (1993) – at the prompting of Russell Sparkes and Sue Ward, a trade union expert on pension law – made it clear that pension funds are allowed to invest ethically as long as no loss is incurred. The Government's Pensions Review now needs to provide individual citizens with the opportunity to put the ethical question to their pension fund managers and to demand changes if necessary.

Statutory change

If the regulators had a statutory duty to require pension fund investors to set out their policy on ethical questions, it would put a new dynamic into the system. In turn, the regulators should encourage the incorporation of clauses into schemes which require ethical questions to be considered. This should be made a fiduciary duty, as much a requirement on trustees and fund managers as the setting out of financial objectives.

The Government is considering index-tracking personal pensions with low charges. They should also track pensions which operate on ethical criteria and look at ways of encouraging venture-capital and long-term investments by pension funds into those companies which have a socially responsible and ethical policy. This will become even more critical as the Government encourages us to rely less on state pensions and more on private ones. Provision needs to be made for advisory ballots to test members' views on major ethical questions.

Make a stand, ask the questions, and make
sure you receive both answers and action.

Big local election issue

Motivated voters can make an issue of investment policies during the annual round of local elections. In an area like Merseyside, for example – where, since the mid-1980s, the pension funds have been administered by Wirral, one of the five district councils – the sum involved has grown to £2.3 billion. Although Wirral's acting director of finance, Ian Colman, tells me that the other four district councils have no direct input, it would be inconceivable that the political representatives on his Pension Committee would not be responsive to demands from their partners about the way in which the money is invested. The representatives in turn should be responsive to the voices of their constituents – so make a stand, ask the questions, and make sure you receive both answers and action.

What is true for Merseyside is true of most of the 99 pension funds administered by local government, but some regions have already developed more enlightened policies.

- Edinburgh City Council uses its status as a shareholder to exert influence on companies behaving badly; it makes fund managers aware of council policies; and allocates about 2 per cent of its total £1.2 billion investment fund to a specialist manager to invest ethically.

- The London Borough of Sutton has operated a policy of socially responsible investment since 1990.

- Kingston and Richmond both have ethical policies.

- Nottingham has commissioned a £60,000 investigation into how its £1 billion pension fund is invested.
- Hampshire, Devon, Derbyshire and Lincolnshire invest a portion of their funds according to ethical or environmental criteria.

Clearly, with vast sums of money at stake, the local government voter, the local political parties, the local councillor and the local government employee are all in a superb position to lobby for funds to be directed in particular ways. An economic vote is likely to have just as much influence as a political vote in shaping priorities. We use our votes in elections to achieve change, so why not use our savings and pensions in the same way?

Private pension funds

For the private pension fund investor opportunities already exist to shop around ethically. EIRIS publishes an independent guide, *Money & Ethics*, which enables investors to select pensions, PEPs, endowment mortgages and unit and investment trusts which mirror their ethical concerns. Covering 32 funds, the guide ranks funds on the basis of positive company activities as well as detailing their negative activities. The public demand for a more ethical approach was mirrored by the recent launch of three new funds – Merchant Investors Assurance Ethical Fund, NPI Global Care Managed Fund, and United Charities Ethical Trust.

We use our votes in elections to achieve change,
so why not use our savings and pensions in
the same way?

Ethical performance

The scoring arrangements which EIRIS has devised for its guide, easy to read and comprehend, make it easy for lay people to test a fund's performance against its declared objectives. As previously commented, rhetoric and performance are not always the same thing. Awarding a score on a scale of one to ten, EIRIS compares the ethical performance of each fund with the overall performance of the FTSE All-Share Index. This easily accessed information is encouraging to investors and is no doubt one of the major reasons why ethical funds grew from £0.7 billion in 1992 to £1.6 billion in 1997, with more than 136,000 people holding policies and units in ethical funds. Properly marketed, future growth could be exponential.

In Chapter 6 of *The Ethical Investor* Russell Sparkes devotes himself to an exploration of the investment performance of ethical funds. He describes fully the study he undertook for the *Institute of Investment Management and Research Journal*. Since then the WM Company, the largest firm of consulting actuaries to the pension fund industry, has produced a study showing that charity investors have reaped positive gains by investing ethically.[6] A major British academic study was published in the *Journal of Business Finance and Accounting* in June 1995.[7] Its conclusion was that 'the ethical trusts tend to outperform the non-ethical ones'.

Rhetoric and performance are not always the same thing.

Before choosing an 'ethical' fund, the consumer needs to know what its managers mean by the word. There is also an argument that in the longer term the funds may not perform so well. The argument is that commercial organizations are using popular concerns to sell investment products to the public. Since the charges on these funds are higher than usual, they are open to the criticism that they are highly profitable for the insurance companies who sell them, but their excessively scrupulous and negative exclusion criteria means that they are likely to perform badly compared to comparable products. Even if they did not perform as well as non-ethical funds, should that in fact be the primary consideration?

It is also argued that such a negative avoidance approach does little to change corporate behaviour. Sometimes *engaging* in a company rather than rejecting it as an investment opportunity may help to influence policy changes (e.g. in the case of the Methodist CFB, Russell Sparkes recommended that they remain engaged in Shell and they are 'now seeing signs of change'[8] within the senior management in respect of their operations in Nigeria – where there were major concerns about human rights abuses, labour conditions and the environment).

Sparkes argues that any fund manager wishing to sell ethical products must carry out two steps to answer these criticisms.[9]

1. There should be an Independent Advisory committee to ask awkward questions of the investors and to ensure that the ethical claims are being respected by both the investors and the companies who have received the investments.

2. They should have some in-house research expertise to investigate ethical issues when they arise.

Many ethical funds have delegated their screening process to EIRIS and do not go out actively looking for ethical issues in their daily investment work. EIRIS do a good job, but they rely on annual company reports. This inevitably makes them reactive not proactive, and if something is not mentioned in a report they may miss it.

By contrast, the approach adopted by Sparkes and the Methodist CFB is proactive. All fund managers are charged with looking out for ethical issues when they analyse or meet with companies. So, for instance, when they noticed that BSkyB was going to broadcast the Playboy Channel, they immediately announced that they were selling their shares because of it. They received global coverage as they trenchantly made their point.

Friends Provident, the Co-operative Insurance Services, Environ and CFB all have their own advisory committees and do their own research, but Sparkes says that the majority of ethical funds do not. This should change.

More than mere altruism

Persuading companies to take these issues more seriously will depend on our ability to get those involved to think with both their hearts and their heads. They will need to be convinced that it is not just a matter of altruism or social responsibility – but good business sense too.

- One American study recorded an average increase of 0.82 per cent in share prices of a company who won environmental awards. This was worth $80 million.[10]
- The same study recorded a cut in share prices of 1.5 per cent (worth $30 million) following an environmental disaster or oil spill.

The cleaning-up of beaches costs less than the reduction in share value. Awareness of the sensibilities of investors has led to financial commentators inventing the new term 'triple bottom line' to describe not just financial performance but also ethical and environmental performance. David Tozer of EIRIS suggests that this triple bottom line will include:

- a basic commitment to an ethical approach, including policy, charters and codes;
- internal audit of performance by management;
- where products are concerned, eco-labelling and an analysis of the products' life-cycle.

Persuading companies to take these issues more seriously will depend on our ability to get those involved to think with both their hearts and their heads.

An ethical mortgage

Apart from pensions and insurance, the other personal financial commitment into which most people enter is a mortgage on a house.

A straightforward repayment mortgage involves a loan to purchase the property and monthly repayment of the capital plus interest. Endowment mortgages, on the other hand, usually involve paying just the interest on the loan. This is invested and at the end of the repayment period the investment will be used to pay off the original purchase price – and to provide a lump sum. Sixty per cent of all mortgages are endowments and they also provide an opportunity for the ethical citizen to act.

Among the companies which are already marketing endowment mortgages with ethical criteria are Equitable Life, Friends Provident and Sovereign Unit Trust Managers. Such ethical funds are now being sought out by new borrowers, but it is also possible for existing mortgage holders to exert pressure on their mortgage company and ask for their investment to be transferred to an ethical fund. The easier this process becomes, the more ordinary people will take advantage of it. As consumers increasingly decide to shop around for ethical reasons, institutions will become more adept at meeting the demand.

Savings initiatives

The Inland Revenue recently undertook a consultation on personal savings. The UK Social Investment Forum has argued that investments in non-profit social finance organizations (companies committed to operating in disadvantaged communities without an expectation of reaping rich rewards) should be included within the Individual Savings Account (ISA) scheme. Although credit union deposits and stocks and shares in Industrial and Provident societies will be eligible, social finance organizations are specifically excluded at present.

Ethical investment and social investment (creating employment projects, for instance, in disadvantaged neighbourhoods) are not in competition and the Government will be making a mistake if it does not rectify this omission. Obsession with market forces should not be the only concern of a Labour Government. It should harness the growing sense of social responsibility within the corporate sector, encourage it with matching money incentives, and not be ashamed of having a heart for the poor.

Stimulus should also be given to more community banks and social banking in the poorer areas from which commercial banks have largely withdrawn. In a city like Liverpool, for example, vast numbers of banks have been closed in down-town districts.

By contrast, in American cities, new community banks have seen extraordinary success and achieved a great deal of good for the neighbourhood.

- European social banking has financed 5,000 social economy projects, invested $1 billion dollars, and has an overall equity base of $34 million.
- US community banks have financed $2.5 billion of economic development and hold a capital reserve base of $800 million.[11]

With these examples to look to, there is huge scope for expanding existing initiatives in the UK, building in particular on the success of the small credit union projects which have mushroomed in many less well-off communities.

Arms and the man

With all these aspects of consumerism and financial investment in mind, another area in which the ethical citizen can make a huge impact is in influencing those companies and countries which sell arms.

Unknowingly and unquestioningly, many people will have their savings wrapped up in companies which are involved in the arms trade.

In the spring of 1997 St Paul's Cathedral sparked controversy by accepting sponsorship from the world's leading arms manufacturer for a concert to be held there that July. Public pressure subsequently encouraged them to reverse their decision. How did such an enormous faux pas come to happen in the first place?

The Church of England has a declared ethical investment policy which includes not investing in armaments, but this argument is neither unique to Anglicans nor without implications for us all. Unknowingly and unquestioningly, many people will have their savings wrapped up in companies which are involved in the arms trade.

We should be aware, and therefore wary, of the strategy of some giant corporations, determined to buy influence and acquire respectability. Persuading well regarded institutions to accept sponsorship from an arms company implies that the company's business has been given a clean bill of health by those accepting the sponsorship – in the case of the cathedral concert, it even implied the sanctity of a church blessing.

Such innocent naivety simply won't do – for any of us.

St Paul's was going to receive £15,000 for their concert. Lockheed Martin Tactical Systems (UK) generates hundreds of millions of pounds in arms sales. They have sold military transporters to such countries as Indonesia, Zaire, Sudan and Nigeria. For a tiny outlay they stood to gain considerable kudos. The sponsorship money was to provide hospitality for the invited guests – who included the major British arms companies British Aerospace and GEC.

The canons of the Cathedral pleaded ignorance: 'I thought Lockheed made engines for aeroplanes,' said one – no doubt entirely sincerely. But such innocent naivety simply won't do – for any of us. What can we do to protect ourselves and fight such deceptive strategy?

Your dirty money

General Booth, the founder of the Salvation Army, once famously remarked: 'Give me your dirty money and I will wash it clean.' Up to a point. It is true, for instance, that parish priests do not know who puts money into their plates and boxes each week, but they nevertheless use that money and put it to good use. That is palpably different, however, from a company with dubious ethics using sponsorship deals to promote their image and their sales.

Institutions should always ensure that large donations are made public and are transparent (so that, as in the case of St Paul's, there is the possibility of reversing a decision if the source is revealed to be an unpalatable one). Investors, collectively and individually, through savings and shares, can inform themselves and decide whether to continue to aid and abet companies who directly trade in death. Individuals acting together do have the power to cause change. And there is a need for change.

Investors can decide whether to continue to aid and abet companies who directly trade in death.

Holes in the bucket

In Britain today there are 2,000 arms factories employing some 500,000 people. For these companies, morality and principles have largely been reduced to the matter of sales. Britain generates an estimated £5 billion per annum through arms sales and ranks as the world's second largest exporter of such goods.

Politicians often use the jobs argument to justify this. Rarely is the possibility of job diversification ever mentioned. The Eurofighter project is a good example. It is claimed that 15,000 jobs depend on the project. The cost of researching, designing and building EFA is put at £15 billion – about £1 million per job. Could these resources not be put to a better use which actually creates more employment more economically? Alan Clark, MP and military historian, put it well when he said: 'We must find a less extravagant way of paying people to make buckets with holes in them.'[12]

New Labour arms ethics

In 1997 the incoming Labour Government proclaimed an 'ethical' foreign policy – just as the Foreign Secretary, Robin Cook, proceeded to renew all 21,000 licences permitting arms exports. Countries which pursued internal oppression or external aggression were meant to have been caught by the policy, but none were. Indeed, 20 new Hawk Ground Attack aircraft and over 300 armoured vehicles were sold to Indonesia – which was responsible for the deaths of 200,000 people in East Timor. The Government subsequently sponsored an Arms Fair at Farnborough, where 300 UK arms companies exhibited their wares. Their customers included Turkey, Saudi Arabia, Indonesia and China. Indonesia's General Wiranto was among their number. He spent a major part of his army career in East Timor and was involved in the invasion and subsequent military action there. Does he subscribe to Labour's 'ethical' code? And if Indonesia does not fall foul of the code, who will?

Government rhetoric and practice must be reconciled. This will only happen when members of the public exert influence through their elected representatives and through companies which rely on their investments. Do not underestimate the effect of public pressure. The Nobel Peace Prize winner Mother Teresa of Calcutta compared the effect of individuals to the drops of water which make up the ocean.

Do not underestimate the effect of public pressure.

I am treasurer of the all-party parliamentary committee opposed to anti-personnel landmines. Although the intervention of Diana, Princess of Wales was to be a defining moment in the campaign to eradicate these appalling weapons, public opinion played an equally crucial part in affecting Government policy. Individual members of the public acting together for the cause were the drops which made up the ocean.

The arms industry at prayer

Individuals, of course, also make up any number of corporate organizations, from trades unions to churches, and they have investments and purchasing policies too: another avenue for ethical citizens to exert pressure.

How many church members have ever bothered to look at where their church invests?

There is no church in Britain which does not oppose the trade in arms. Yet how many church members have ever bothered to look at where their church invests – or done anything about it? Look at these figures. According to the Campaign Against the Arms Trade (CATT):

- The Dean and Chapter at Liverpool Cathedral owned more than 200,000 shares in Lucas.
- The Church of England Pension Fund held 233,000 shares in GEC.
- The Church Commissioners held 3 million shares in GEC and nearly as many in Lucas.
- The YMCA held 13,000 shares in GEC and 19,000 in Lucas.
- Jewish Care held 71,000 shares in GEC.
- The Presbyterian Church of Ireland held 109,000 shares in GEC.

This was the situation in 1996, and dozens more are listed. Some of these church groups sold their shareholdings after being contacted by CATT; others became involved in investor action. The Church Commissioners of the Church of England met with the senior management of GEC to raise ethical concerns over some of the company's activities. GEC's arms production is now below 30 per cent of their total production (though GEC certainly makes no virtue of this and Church sources have not claimed responsibility for influencing policy). This is an improvement, but nonetheless prompts the question: is sin permissible because a person remains virtuous for the other 70 per cent of the time? The Laws of Moses and the Ten Commandments would seem banal if we were told that keeping seven out of ten commandments would suffice. There is some way to go yet. Ethical citizens must hold onto their values and keep the pressure up.

Seize the moment

In 1863 Abraham Lincoln warned his nation: 'We have grown in power and wealth as no other nation has grown. But ... intoxicated with unbroken success, we have become too self-suffcient to feel the necessity of redeeming and preserving grace.' He urged them to change.

Carpe diem, seize the moment, so the old Latin saying advised. In seizing the moment we should understand that many of our citizens want more than the intoxication of wealth, that they do not wish to be just a money-making mob. Many of us want change and a reconsideration of the values at the heart of our society. The moment has arrived to take action and press for ethical values to be reclaimed and upheld in every area of life, perhaps most especially in business and financial dealings.

Essential Questions

- Have you ever written to a company either encouraging or criticizing them for their employment practices or investment policy?

- If you have any personal savings or investments, have you considered their ethical implications? Would you do so in the future?

- Would you want your savings to be used in the production of armaments, the promotion of abortion, the exploitation of children, the degradation of the environment, or the abuse of human rights?

- Do you know how your local Council invests its funds? Can you find out if the Councillors have an ethical investment policy?

- Does your chosen charity, voluntary organization or church have investments in dubious companies?

- Do you think Government could do more to promote ethical and social investment?

3/ Citizen Discernment

As the previous two chapters have shown, individual choice rather than the common good has been relentlessly promoted in recent decades. The consequences are all around us. Discerning citizens will soon recognize that the cult of individualism and material prosperity is not enough for a fulfilled life. In fact, it breeds its own cycle of disappointment. Like the ancient Greeks who finally climbed Mount Olympus to search out their gods, modern men and women have scaled the peaks of prosperity and found nothing there. Often they feel cheated – having sought the truth, they have been offered only lies.

How do we educate ourselves to deal with all the dilemmas presented by modern living? Does our education system go any way towards preparing us to be discerning citizens?

Little children, little problems

The old saying, 'Give me a child until he's seven and I'll give you a man for life', reminds us that the early, formative years are crucial to each individual's personal development. I argued in Chapter 1 that dysfunctional families and absentee parents may have a devastating effect on a small child. Children can feel rootless and become out of control if they are not provided with secure and loving guidance from parents right through their developing years.

'Little children, little problems; big children, big problems' is a description which sums up the challenge for parents to be loving but firm. Think of the consequences. Showering children with expensive presents or dumping them in front of the television is no substitute for spending time doing things *with* them, nor is it an effective way of teaching (by example) respect and consideration for others. Children thrive on love and constructive attention.

Parents remain a child's best teacher.

While I was a City Councillor and MP, I frequently went into constituents' homes. It is true that there were pockets of desperate material poverty, but I was often struck by the fact that even where there was a good income and material affluence, some homes were spiritually and culturally poor. I cannot be alone in mourning the replacement of the hearth by the flickering box in the corner as the focal point of the living room, or the loss of shared conversation around a meal table. These are the places and times when children learn – and parents remain a child's best teacher.

Homes without books

I have also been struck by the complete absence of books in some people's homes. It is never too early to read to a child – yet many parents do not buy books and many homes are devoid of them.

Albert Einstein said that if you want a brilliant child you should simply give them good story books to read: 'If you want your children to be brilliant tell them fairy tales.' Instead, many children are not read to or read with – and subsequent literacy and discipline problems stem from this. Youth workers regularly tell me that most crime in their neighbourhoods is committed by school truants. The truants are often children who have reached secondary school without the ability to read or write, and who frequently have a low sense of self-esteem. When they do attend school, these are the children who present the biggest disciplinary problems to teachers, who then spend more time policing than teaching.

Truants are often children who have reached secondary school without the ability to read or write.

More time invested in literacy skills might bring better returns than 'boot camps', curfews and other punitive measures. So might some interest in the materials to which children are being exposed.

What children are getting sight of often beggars belief. Instead of being taught, challenged and delighted by the best of an enormous range of English literature (both old and modern) many of the texts used in schools today seem to be quite extraordinary choices.

- 14-year-old GCSE English pupils were given a book in which a teenager has an abortion after being gang-raped and the foetus is incinerated alive.[1]
- An eight-year-old in Trafford borrowed a school library book called *The Wheatstone Pond*, written by an award-winning children's author. The book contains foul language and is explicit about rape, contraceptives, and the murder of a young boy who is cut up and flushed down the toilet.
- The Outstanding Children's Book of the Year Award in 1994 included on its shortlist a book called *Johnny and the Dead* by Terry Pratchett. The story involves a 12-year-old boy who communes with the corpses in a cemetery. Although Pratchett's stories are by no means the worst offenders – and are not awash with foul language and violence – can't we create more positive storylines?
- Another shortlisted book for the same award, *Head and Tails*, is the story of two children who cut off the head of their dead father and boil it in a cauldron.

Is this really the kind of material we want our children to be reading? Does this sort of 'education' create discernment? Does it help to protect the innocence of childhood?

Unfolding truths

There will, of course, always be a place in literature for the macabre and even the grotesque. Roald Dahl is the best exponent of this, with some genuinely off-beat and funny tales. But should we be filling young children's minds with a surfeit of stories which are also vicious and entirely negative?

A few years ago the *Daily Telegraph* reviewed a selection of children's books for its Book Week. The reviewer described 'covers with clawing hands, scary toys, dripping blood, laughing masks. Violence, fear and the occasional touch of fantasy, it appeared, were the only genres with appeal.'[2] What a contrast with the likes of John Buchan, or Arthur Ransome, or the stories of J.R.R. Tolkien and his contemporary C.S. Lewis. Both Tolkien and Lewis use fantasy and evil images, sometimes to chilling effect, but always in the context of the ultimate triumph of good over evil.

Should we be filling young children's minds with a surfeit of stories which are vicious and entirely negative?

Early childhood should be a time of unfolding truths. There is enough time later on for the adult world. Surely we should be trying to protect this gentle time of innocence – as untroubled by the darker side of life as is humanly possible. If children are not given time to *be* children, to form the values and skills which will balance their lives in the future, what will the consequences be? These are already becoming clear.

Instead of first learning the art of discernment, children have become confused as adult ideas are thrust upon them too early – often causing terrible shock and disorientation. Contemporary culture has invaded the imaginations of young children and robbed them of the wonders and beauty of childhood. In place of innocence they are filled with a diet of nastiness and vulgarity – and then we throw up our hands in horror when they do nasty or vulgar things. We complain that they do not have our values – but if we look around us, we can see all too plainly that those values are precisely what they do have.

Tragically, such is the pressure to conform, the child who has the guts to reject the diet of vulgarity and buck the trends of his or her peers is frequently mocked. In our mixed-up world we have inverted the true virtues and traditional values. Where is our own discernment now? Why are we letting the precious years of childhood be destroyed?

No longer children

Pressurized children of the 1990s hardly dare refer to themselves as 'children' any more: all too soon they enter the world of adult realities and adult choices. Rosemary Anne Sisson, the children's author, expressed it well when she said: 'The number of young who regard their childhood as a joyful time of fun has shrunk to the lowest point this century. The most innocent of children when I was growing up knew a good deal about death and suffering. The difference is that they did not revel in it, nor were they expected to be horrified by it.'[3] She is right. We have made an art form of horror and dress up the macabre as entertainment. Why are we surprised that our children's sense of fun and innocence has been destroyed?

If a child is culturally and spiritually impoverished before he or she even begins school, a teacher's job will be extraordinarily difficult. Children who are allowed to run amok at home sense that they are unloved and consequently have no feeling of security or rootedness. An unfocused, unencouraged child becomes unmotivated and all the discipline problems which turn teachers into policemen flow from this. The development of responsible behaviour is impossible unless parents actively help to shape their children's wills.

An unfocused, unencouraged child becomes unmotivated.

Some children seem to emerge from the womb with truculence and mischief written across their faces. Dr James Dobson has written engagingly on this phenomenon and what you can do about it.[4] The tug of war which all parents have with their young children often leaves them exhausted – I can tell you that political battles with parliamentary lags stubbornly defending the establishment pale into insignificance by comparison – but the battle must be waged. Dr Dobson says 'the defiant youngster is in a "high risk" category for antisocial behaviour later in life'. If this is to be avoided, the wilfulness has to be channelled creatively. The foundations for creating discerning, responsible citizens are laid early in life, in those formative childhood years. These are the vital steps parents must take to guide their child's development:

- Define boundaries.
- Be decisive and consistent when the boundaries are challenged.
- Reassure and teach the child once a confrontation is over, carefully explaining why certain behaviour is unacceptable.
- Nurture the child to respect rules and to show consideration for others.
- Encourage a sense of responsibility and duty.
- Rewards acts of kindness, consideration and generosity.
- Explain the obligations each person has to their family and wider community.

An organized environment

Children need an organized environment at home and at school. This need not be repressive, rigid or unbearably harsh: wills need to be shaped not crushed. But if a child is not formed at home in a secure environment where the boundaries are clear, a teacher's job becomes far more difficult.

The idea that children somehow suffer because their parents show them loving leadership is nothing less than absurd. Leaving children to 'find their own way' and abandoning parental authority to *laissez-faire* philosophies is in some ways another form of child neglect. This may seem like very strong language, but children can be damaged for life if they are deprived of guidance or always left 'to make their own mistakes'. In many of our overspill estates and inner cities, for example (although the problem is far from being confined to these areas), there are droves of unloved, unguided children roaming the streets. They have little idea of what is expected of them, or of why their behaviour is anti-social. The complete absence of fathers from many of their lives hardly helps their personal development.

From generation to generation, families remain the best and most appropriate place in which to transmit values and beliefs.

Just as absurd is the wrong-headed notion that parents have no rights or obligations to instil their values, attitudes or beliefs in their children. In the Bible, Solomon understood this well when he told parents to 'Train a child in the way he should go; and when he is old he will not depart from it' (Proverbs 22:6). From generation to generation, families remain the best and most appropriate place in which to transmit values and beliefs.

As I said in Chapter 1, we should never underestimate the importance of the extended family in shaping a child. Aunts, uncles and grandparents have probably never read any of the textbooks on parenting which are so prolifically available today, let alone attended courses on parenting or counselling, yet their acquired common sense, experience and wisdom make them an indispensable part of what a child needs for a rounded education which will prepare them for life. Spare us from the industry of 'experts' and 'professionals' who have largely taken their place. Without the streetwise knowledge of the extended family, parenting becomes an isolated, hit-and-miss business. It is no wonder that it so often ends in tears.

Catastrophic loss

In his book *After Virtue*, Alisdair MacIntyre identifies the disintegrated nature of contemporary society.[5] He says that we have reached the point where we no longer realize the nature of the catastrophe we have suffered. In dismantling the extended family, with all its educational, cultural and social support systems, we have been visited by a catastrophe which we have hardly noticed.

MacIntyre argues that 'the academic curriculum would turn out to be among the symptoms of the disaster whose occurrence the curriculum does not acknowledge'.

He asserts that the most striking feature of contemporary moral debate is that it largely centres upon disagreements: 'There seems no rational way of securing moral agreement in our culture.' This has created a crisis within our families and even more so within our schools.

No one is sure any longer about what they should teach a child. They are frightened of being too 'prescriptive'. Teachers and parents are frightened to present marriage and strong families as ideals, or to challenge contemporary culture, and Judaeo-Christian values may only be referred to as just another brand on the shelf – 'You have your values, I have mine.' Is it any wonder that confusion is rife?

'Men without chests'

The 'value neutral' education which many schools now deliver has been developed by those whom C.S. Lewis variously described as 'the conditioners' and 'the men without chests'.[6] Lewis said it was an outrage that they 'should be commonly spoken of as Intellectuals'. What Lewis was getting at was that society demands all the virtues – courage, self-sacrifice, generosity and the rest – but its educators have no ability to deliver these qualities. He sums it up by saying, 'In a sort of ghastly simplicity we remove the organ and demand the function. We make men without chests and expect of them virtue and enterprise. We laugh at honour and are shocked to find traitors in our midst. We castrate and bid the geldings be fruitful.'

Too much of the debate about education recently has centred on league tables and methods of assessment. Too little has been said about the sort of citizens we are producing. As Lewis said, how can we expect a gelding to be fruitful? If we deny children education and formation in the commonly held values vital to an ordered and se-cure society, what chance will they have to become discerning? There is also a clear link with academic standards. If children have no concept of responsibility or respect, duty or obligation, their behaviour fatally disrupts the life and achievements of the whole school. These are the primary reasons why we must begin actively to educate for citizenship. The chance to stem the tide is slipping away.

Too much of the debate about education recently has centred on league tables and methods of assessment. Too little has been said about the sort of citizens we are producing.

The task of education

The task of education as a whole should be to form discerning citizens, people who will act for others, people who will ultimately have a love of the world around them and feel responsibility towards it.

For most young people civic education (i.e. an understanding of communal responsibilities and how democracy functions) is generally acquired incidentally, through contacts with voluntary projects, or the occasional teacher who sees it as important, or through an event or political policy which touches them personally. We must be far more systematic than this and ask tough questions which demand tough answers and definite action.

- What is the purpose of education?
- Do our schools fulfil this purpose?
- What is expected of democratic citizens?
- Do we meet these expectations?
- What skills do we require to live peaceably together?
- Are we teaching these skills effectively to our young people?

Educating for citizenship

In 1882 Arnold Toynbee, addressing a meeting of the Co-operative Union, made a telling speech about adult education. He called for 'education of the citizen'. At the same time there was a flurry of publications on the subject, such as Professor John MacCunn's *The Ethics of Citizenship* and *The Principles of Citizenship* by Sir Henry Jones. A host of Liberal statesmen, including H.A.L. Fisher and A.H.D. Acland, also wrote about the subject and in France *la morale civique* was developed under the leadership of the sociologist Emile Durkheim.

All this activity was aimed at those to whom the franchise had recently been extended. Although it was a minority pastime, it gradually cultivated a generation of people who took their civic responsibilities very seriously.

People were encouraged to enter local politics, to work in voluntary organizations, and to practise self-help. Educationalists were encouraged to support movements to establish provincial universities, to open their own foundations to those who had been previously excluded, and to admit women. This earnestness and so-called Educational Idealism encouraged individual effort, a distrust of top-down initiatives (are we not once again suffering from a surfeit of centralization in modern Britain?), and direct contact with the disadvantaged. It was the coupling of theory and practice.

Better and longer education feeds back into the community, while lack of education and training denies social status and breeds alienation and estrangement.

It is often said that educational reformers have overexaggerated the benefits of extending high-quality education. Experience proves otherwise. High-quality education nurtures high-quality leaders. Better and longer education feeds back into the community, while lack of education and training denies social status and breeds alienation and estrangement. Those writing in the late 1880s were concerned with the principles for adult education, but the benefits of high-quality education are just as, if not more, important for young people of school age.

A duty to educate

As well as being a poet, Matthew Arnold was a leading nineteenth-century social and educational commentator (he was also a schools inspector for 35 years), and he argued forcefully that there was no need more urgent than a coherent and effective system of schooling. Arnold believed that the State has an over-riding duty to make provision for education, 'in the name of an interest wider than that of individuals',[7] i.e. in the interests of the common good. Voluntary action certainly has a role to play, but when that is not enough, the State must provide the means. Any professed faith in citizenship should incorporate the principles of equality of opportunity and justice, ensuring that a ladder of learning is available to everyone who wishes to climb it.

How can we expect our children to succeed
if we do not give them the means?

Anyone with a shred of respect or pride for their country – or simply a concern for the future – must surely agree that the way we prepare the next generation is of supreme importance. At the very least our young people need the basic tools of literacy and numeracy which will allow them to extend their knowledge and to understand the world around them. We must also teach them how to be good citizens. By not teaching even these basics effectively, we are hobbling the next generation and placing vast roadblocks on their way towards leading fulfilled lives as discerning citizens. How can we expect our children to succeed if we do not give them the means?

Government moves

At long last the need to educate for citizenship has been recognized by the Government and a White Paper has been produced.[8] The Secretary of State for Education, David Blunkett, was a member of the groundbreaking Speaker's Commission 'Encouraging Citizenship' in 1990 chaired by Lord Weatherill, which declared: 'Citizenship should be a part of every young person's education from the earliest years of schooling and continuing into the post-school years within further and higher education.' The White Paper itself states: 'Schools can help to ensure that young people feel that they have a stake in our society and the community in which they live by teaching them the nature of democracy and the duties, responsibilities and rights of citizens.'

In response to the White Paper, I wrote in *The Times* that 'one of the casualties of the pell mell rush towards a more individualistic approach has been civic responsibility. Looking out for "number one" has had a poisonous effect as individualism encourages people to opt out and to privatise their lives – becoming limited by the narrow confines of their job or their home. Only in Britain would we turn "community service" into a punishment dispensed by magistrates.'[9]

The role of education in the formation of good citizens became a central concern for Mrs Frances Lawrence following the tragic death of her husband, Philip, outside his London school. National introspection also followed the killing of James Bulger and the Dunblane massacre. Frances Lawrence's personal manifesto was published in *The Times* on 21 October 1996. She set out her aims as being:

- the establishment of a nationwide movement to banish violence and to encourage civic values;
- a ban on the sale of combat knives and the closure of shops that stock them;
- primary school lessons in good citizenship;
- the raising of the status of police and teachers;
- the end of government neutrality on the family;
- parents who would no longer allow children to lead separate lives within the home;
- an emphasis on teaching the three Es – effort, earnestness and excellence.

A number of publications over recent years have reinforced this growing awareness of the need for education in citizenship, including David Selbourne's *The Principle of Duty*, Amitai Etzioni's *The Spirit of Community* and two books by the Chief Rabbi Dr Jonathan Sacks, *The Politics of Hope* and *Faith in the Future*. How far will the Government go in meeting public concern over the situation?

League table limitations

If all that emerges from this current debate about citizenship is another series of miserable little charters linked to consumerism, choice, entitlements and rights, it will be a tragically wasted opportunity.

An obsession with league tables and assessments has led to our failure to appreciate the role of education in fostering a civilized society, in the formation of discerning citizens, in the cultivation of true virtue, and in the pursuit of the common good. We have become so focused on results that we have forgotten the purpose.

Aristotle, with all the wisdom of Plato before him, could find no better definition of the true good for man than the full exercise of the soul's faculties in accordance with its proper excellence. In other words, of what use is material or even academic attainment if it is not placed at the service of others? Is this not how we achieve true satisfaction and true happiness? Aristotle said that we had to educate for virtue and this is no different today.

If all that emerges is another series of miserable little charters linked to consumerism, choice, entitlements and rights, it will be a tragically wasted opportunity.

In *The City of History*, written in the 1960s, Lewis Mumford perceptively and prophetically saw how the balance of civil society can be threatened by a failure to take education seriously:

> Before modern man can gain control over the forces that now threaten his very existence, he must resume possession of himself. This sets the chief mission for the city of the future: that of creating a visible regional and civic structure, designed to make man at home with his deeper self and his larger world, attached to images of human nature and love. We must now conceive the city, accordingly, not primarily as a place of business or government, but as an essential organ for expressing and actualising the new human personality.[10]

Mumford saw the need to address the question of human development and personal expression. He appreciated the scale of de-industrialization which would occur in later years, the social problems which would flow from this and the need to invest heavily in education as a re-balancing measure: 'Not industry, but education will be the centre of their [the cities'] activities,' he wrote.[11]

Surely such education should never be limited to the kind of learning which can be measured in simplistic league tables and examination results? As H.G. Wells said: 'Maintaining civilisation is a constant race between education and catastrophe.'[12]

Self-knowledge and self-worth

The education of the citizen should ideally underline the moral significance of self-knowledge and self-worth. I am constantly surprised by the very low sense of self-esteem which many young people have. This is compounded by a sense of helplessness, a belief that nothing they say or do will make any difference. We must all learn to appreciate ourselves as moral agents in the way we live and affect others. Only then can we truly develop the art of discernment.

Without such an appreciation we end up justifying our actions by the unthinking assertion that we were 'only obeying orders' or that 'it's what everyone else does'. This simply is not enough. In an ordered, secure society, each individual must be able to discern right from wrong, and take responsibility for his or her actions. In extreme cases an inability to do so can lead to the atrocities of the concentration camps, to the nightmare kingdoms of Nazism and communism, to apartheid and totalitarianism. More commonplace examples are around us every day, ranging from bad neighbours to litter louts.

---

*Part of educating for citizenship is
educating us to know ourselves.*

Agents for change

Unless discerning citizens are able to conceive of themselves as agents – as personally capable of affecting other people and events – it will be impossible to develop any sense of responsibility or judgement. The teaching of rules must genuinely serve the process of developing discernment and judgement. Simply being told that stealing or lying is wrong, for example, is not enough: we need to know what it is about them that makes them wrong or unacceptable.

Part of educating for citizenship is educating us to know ourselves. Without self-knowledge we cannot properly control our desires, combat temptations, cope with our failures and inadequacies, or learn how to react to provocation. Even such a great man as Dietrich Bonhoeffer, contemplating his execution by the Nazis, wrote about his weaknesses. This self-knowledge ultimately gave him the inner strength he needed to stand against Hitler. He was confident in his own moral judgement.

It is true that there are moral judgements about which there will be different conclusions, such as capital punishment, hunting or abortion. Never the less, we do need honest debate about these dilemmas within our homes and our schools, in the media and in politics. Some commonly shared principles may at least be agreed, such as a common love of democracy or a common abhorrence of cruelty. Teasing out the areas of agreement is as important as registering the disagreements. Children should be allowed to hear the arguments *in favour of* acquiring knowledge, cherishing the family, or upholding the sanctity of human life, as well as the negative angles on these values with which they are constantly bombarded.

The eighteenth-century statesman and political theorist Edmund Burke counselled that a liberal society required a moral citizenry. When self-control was developed through conscience, character, habit or religion, it would reduce the need for the State to resort to punitive or coercive measures: 'Men are qualified for civil liberty in exact proportion to their disposition to put moral chains upon their own appetites,' he wrote in 1791.[13]

Burke also said that 'manners are more important than laws'.[14] Perhaps he might have said the same about education league tables. Where do we learn to control our appetites and to cultivate our manners if not at home and at school? The emphasis of modern education has gone badly awry.

Mastering manners

Manners may 'maketh the man', but Thomas More went even further in his classic work, *Utopia*, published in 1516. Not only did his visionary utopian community of Amaurote have representative structures and homes with street doors and garden doors (i.e. everything was to be ordered and families given security and privacy), in More's imaginary city the whole community were 'to withdraw as much time as possible from the service of the body and devote it to the freedom of the mind'. More well understood the civilizing effect of education.

In *The Life of Thomas More*,[15] Peter Ackroyd describes More's strong sense of public duty, which he says was an integral part of his education and parental expectation. In addition, he writes of the man who held such power in the great offices of State – Lord Chancellor and Speaker of the House of Commons – that 'at no point did it ever come into conflict with his instinctive piety; indeed, it was an aspect of it'.

Where do we learn to control our appetites and to cultivate our manners if not at home and at school?

By contrast with Amaurote, modern man – *homo citizen*, if you like – has now mastered every creature above the realm of bacteria and viruses, but he has still not mastered himself. It is only through education and the development of a moral conscience aware of the common good that we have any real hope of conquering the aberrations which destroy civil society. The tendency towards absolute power manifests itself in the guise of the playground bully and the neighbourhood thug as well as the totalitarian despot. In the modern world, absolute power should be consigned to the same dustbin as magic, superstition, or human sacrifice.

Out of control

It does not take much discernment to see that our contemporary society is speeding almost out of control like a gigantic motor car. If it lurches completely out of control, civic life will be left in a crumpled heap by the roadside with no hope of repair. Only through education can we learn the basic skills required to keep the 'car' on the road – and the more subtle nuances which can improve the journey immeasurably.

In the decades since Lewis Mumford argued for heavy investment in education, however, individual prosperity and material greed have been far higher priorities. We have been failing our young people and the community in general, at several levels:

- The national curriculum fails to address the meaning of citizenship and the role of citizens in modern society at any level (dry-as-dust 'civics' courses are certainly not doing the job).
- Industry has failed to cultivate any kind of coherent ethical or socially responsible approach. There is little to hold up to tomorrow's workers as a good example of right practice.
- The community at large shows a general lack of understanding about what a citizen's duties are in a modern democratic state.

Failure to address this lack of commitment to civic matters will have dire consequences. As the next generations of adults grow up, the result can only be further civic disengagement and dysfunction. Why should they bother to put right things they do not even realize are wrong? If they have not been taught, how should they know?

The education debate in recent years has tended to revolve around political rhetoric promising 'more choice'. The demands of the educational establishment have merely been to 'give us more money and trust us'. It has been a losing strategy with the wrong focus.

Focus on children

Focusing on schools rather than the children in them is disastrous. Particularly in the cities, education was once the key to getting out of poverty. Now it is the key that locks the poor in. Selection by the ability to pass an examination (an arbitrary enough yardstick in itself) has been replaced by selection by the ability to buy a house in the correct area – i.e. an area where the schools succeed (usually a more prosperous part of the city) rather than an area where they fail (often the poorer part). Rather than looking at the best ways of developing children's individual aptitudes, they have simply been ghetto-ized, and many have been held back from developing to their full potential.

In the autumn of 1997 I was in the United States and was horrified by how some children seem to get locked into a no-hope neighbourhood. The problems in the States are compounded by the rising levels of violence generated by the gun culture. According to one survey, 135,000 children in America now take guns to school.[16] I was taken to an area of Philadelphia where six children from one school had died in shootings (outside the school premises) during the previous 12 months. In the aftermath of the mass shooting at the school in Jonesboro in 1998, the Governor of Arkansas remarked that if you fill the minds of children with violence, something like that is bound to happen.

An uneducated adult, unqualified for a job,
often turns to crime and frequently fails to
realize his or her potential as a citizen.

There are some stern lessons for us in these experiences and certainly some research undertaken in Pennsylvania on its prison population has application to the UK. In Pennsylvania the prison population has more than quadrupled since 1980. The research showed that well over 75 per cent of prisoners had no high-school education. An uneducated adult, unqualified for a job, often turns to crime and frequently fails to realize his or her potential as a citizen. Socially the results are disastrous; economically they are not too bright either, as potential tax-payers become tax-takers. All the more reason, therefore, to get hold of children early and help to develop their confidence, self-esteem and a respect for those around them. What action can we take to encourage this?

Service learning

One project which has taken off in the States is 'service learning'. Through the Literacy Corps thousands of American undergraduates spend some of their time on an individual basis with children struggling with literacy and numeracy. This achieves several very worthwhile objectives.

- The student receives academic accreditation for the work.
- The child receives much needed practical help.
- The university is brought within the personal experience of children who have probably never met an undergraduate before, thus raising their sights.
- The students' eyes are opened to a world of which they may previously have been blissfully unaware ('town' very often never meets 'gown' in the great university cities).

Towards the end of 1997 I chaired a meeting in Wembley at which some of those responsible for the service learning initiative in Philadelphia discussed its possible application in Britain. Community Service Volunteers and some universities, such as Liverpool John Moores, already have service learning projects up and running. The potential for their growth, and for the good which they could do, must be enormous. John Moores University is pioneering a Diploma in Citizenship, available to any of its students who become involved in the service learning project or another worthwhile community project. Others who will qualify for the diploma include the several hundred students involved on placements in local companies through Business Bridge. By using their skills and initiative, they have helped strengthen the industrial base of the city whilst making useful links which may lead to employment opportunities later on.

Good citizenship awards

The Government could also do worse than look at broadening the use of the schools-based good citizenship awards which have been pioneered in Liverpool by the John Moores University Foundation for Citizenship.

Merseyside has about six hundred primary and secondary schools within its five constituent boroughs. I contacted local companies, asking whether they would be prepared to sponsor an award for good citizenship in each school. At the time of writing, more than 400 schools have sponsors.

Children who win the award are presented with a bronze sculpture by the local Liverpool sculptor Stephen Broadbent. It carries the legend 'Men and women for others' and also bears the name of the school and the sponsoring company. MTL, the local bus company, for instance, has sponsored every school in Knowsley, while Liverpool has seen its schools sponsored by a whole range of enterprises, from the Bank of England to Rapid, a local DIY centre. North West Water have sponsored schools in Wirral and Sefton Chamber of Commerce are promoting the awards in their borough. A representative of the sponsoring company visits the school to make the award (presented annually) – creating a relationship which hopefully will bear other fruits in the future. Each winner also receives an official certificate of recognition from the university.

The first nomination came from an inner-city school in the Everton district. Campion School had received some unhelpful criticism from inspectors about academic standards – but little practical help. The nomination for the citizenship award proved that schools are definitely not solely about academic results.

One of their 12-year-old boys had, since his primary school days, been bringing lunch to his friend who suffers from cerebral palsy. He unfailingly spends the break-time with him and navigates him around the building to his lessons. It is a simple story, but a great example of friendship and concern for someone else. The boy was also discerning enough to see that the physical qualities which the world holds so dear are not what makes for a whole person and are not a necessary requirement for a good friendship.

The fact that the nominations come from their peers means a great deal to the nominees, but it can also prove a great morale booster to the school as a whole.

Another school, Holly Lodge, told me that when they received my letter they groaned inwardly at having to perform yet another task. Nonetheless, a note was put around the school asking for the names of any children who might qualify for the award. From a school of 1,400 pupils, they received 600 nominations. The teacher responsible for the scheme told me they were staggered by the things they learnt about their own pupils – one youngster had taught herself sign language so that she could communicate with a friend who could not hear or speak.

The fact that the nominations come from their peers means a great deal to the nominees, but it can also prove a great morale booster to the school as a whole, encouraging a greater sense of self-worth and self-esteem.

The local newspaper, *The Liverpool Echo*, has also been a partner in the project and has given coverage to youngsters who have received nominations. This has the further advantage of providing some genuine 'good news' stories to counterbalance the never-ending bad news which the papers inevitably report. It may also give some people pause to reflect on the unheard-of goodness in many of our young people, going some way to redressing the image of cities like Liverpool – which are always in the news when something awful happens, but rarely see their positive achievements reported.

Town and gown lectures

The awards are constructive in themselves, but they also need to be backed up by a systematic attempt to educate for democracy and citizenship – to give young people the ability to be discerning, confident, ethical, responsible and active. The Liverpool John Moores University has therefore started to develop teaching materials for this, as well as holding a series of 'town and gown' lectures, open to both the campus and the city. Hundreds of people have been attending.

Held at Liverpool Town Hall and the city's Bluecoat Chambers, the Roscoe Lectures are named for one of the three Liverpool businessmen who, in 1823, founded the Mechanics' Library. From that seed has sprung the vigorous John Moores University, which now boasts some 20,000 students.

William Roscoe's formal education ended at the age of 12, but he spent his whole life expanding his mind and knowledge. He briefly served in Parliament and stood four-square with his friend William Wilberforce against the slave trade that dominated the commerce of his city. He stands at the head of Liverpool's nineteenth-century tradition of philanthropy and public service, and regularly endowed institutions dedicated to education.[17] The Liverpool historian

Ramsay Muir said of Roscoe: 'No native resident has done more to elevate the character of the community, by uniting the successful pursuit of literature and art with the ordinary duties of the citizen and man of business.'[18]

Citizenship has to be experienced and it has to be learnt. Education cannot be a value-free zone.

Roscoe would undoubtedly have approved of the lecture series named for him and dedicated to good citizenship. Contributors have included Stephen Dorrell MP, Martin Bell MP, the BBC broadcaster Martyn Lewis, Frank Field MP, Baroness Williams of Crosby, the Irish President Mary McAleese, the Chief Rabbi Dr Jonathan Sacks, Lord Jenkins, David Blunkett MP, Jack Straw MP, Ann Widdecombe MP, and the university's Vice Chancellor Professor Peter Toyne – whose idea it was to establish the university's Foundation for Citizenship. HarperCollins are publishing the series of lectures as a companion to *Citizen Virtues* and Granada Television have recorded the lectures for use in schools.[19]

Top priority

As all the initiatives described above recognize, citizenship has to be experienced and it has to be learnt. Education *cannot* be a value-free zone. There are many shared assumptions about what makes for a good and stable society. Why be embarrassed to teach children what these are? For each citizen to play their proper part, it is vital that they have the ability to discern the difference between right and wrong, good and bad, and recognize their own responsibility to act accordingly. That should be our top priority within our homes and schools.

Essential Questions

- If you have children, do you surround them with books and help them to read?
- Are you discriminating about what you and your children watch on television?
- Do you provide clear boundaries for behaviour both at home and at school?
- Do you think it is right to leave your children to 'make their own mistakes', or are you prepared to spend time nurturing their ability to discern and make ethical judgements?
- How (if at all) are your local schools educating for citizenship?
- Would you be willing to pressurize your local politicians to implement Frances Lawrence's agenda?
- Are there opportunities to set up service learning schemes and good citizenship awards in your neighbourhood?

4/ Citizen Confidence

The pressure to conform is phenomenal. Advertisers and other vested interests are constantly trying to bamboozle us into thinking this or buying that. It is surprising that more young people are not driven into a life of crime – enticed as they are into believing that in order to be fulfilled they need any number of accessories and possessions.

Peer-group pressure is especially difficult for young people to manage – they need considerable courage to take a contrary view or reject a proposed course of action. It is possible, however, if they can learn to be sure of themselves and certain of their values – if they are encouraged to think through the issues and decide what they believe is right. This applies just as much to adults as young people. It is never too late to start thinking.

I want to affirm the confident citizen who is prepared to swim against the tide. We are not making it easy for people to stand up and be counted for what they believe is right. In a world of new orthodoxies and political correctness taking a stand may well carry a price. As long as you speak out against far-away injustices or in favour of foxes, you will be reasonably well received. Dare to exercise free speech in favour of an unborn child or against drugs, for instance, and you may find your friends and colleagues turning on you.

What are we doing to our children?

How have we allowed this pressure to conform, this pressure not to speak out, to take over? Instead of creating the climate in which young people can maintain their self-respect and develop their confidence, we have destroyed their innocence and stunted their personal growth.

We are not making it easy for people to stand up and be counted for what they believe is right.

The Manchester-based Maranatha Community have carefully documented the consequences of this for Britain's children.[1] Their findings, along with data compiled by other organizations and publications involved with children and young people, help explain why so many young people have no confidence in themselves or in anyone else.

Standing up to the bully

Among the findings were figures showing that one in four pupils suffer bullying at primary and middle schools, whilst the situation in many secondary schools is even more appalling. One schoolgirl of 12 hanged herself following taunting by schoolmates about her red hair. In another tragedy a 13-year-old hanged himself because he was frightened of another youngster.

Children's lives are frequently made an absolute misery as bullying and criminal activity invades their school. Of course this undermines the victims' feelings of security and confidence in themselves. And what about others who see what is going on? It takes a great deal of confidence to stand up to a bully – or to defend another child who is being victimized and brutalized by a gang.

If there is something wrong, then young people should be encouraged to speak out about it to the authorities, or even make an issue of it in the wider community: it is not only adults who have freedom of speech. Only through proper formation and moral guidance can young people develop the necessary confidence, however.

It takes a great deal of confidence to stand up to a bully – or to defend another child who is being victimized and brutalized by a gang.

In practical terms, this means that they need more help to develop skills in formulating arguments, public speaking, using the media, and expressing opinions. These are much neglected areas these days, and young people are consequently left feeling inarticulate and helpless, even if they feel strongly about a particular issue.

As a schoolboy I set up my own, rather badly produced, newspaper. It was an early lesson in how to get my views across. In my student union I learned to move motions and put arguments. As a young Councillor I found out how to get things done in a local community, and as a back-bench MP I was sometimes able to get some minor injustice put right simply by being a persistent, bloody-minded nuisance. But then, I was always fortunate that there were older people around to encourage me and develop my confidence in speaking out. Many young people do not have that privilege today.

Beyond the school gates

Beyond the school gates survival may be even more precarious. Fifty per cent of those found guilty of criminal offences in the United Kingdom today are under the age of 21, while the Home Office estimates that youth crime costs the country more than £7 billion a year.

It is incredibly difficult for young people not to get sucked in by crime. We tantalize them with materialism but often deny them any honest means of earning the money to obtain the things they are told they 'must have'. Others have never been given any guidance on acceptable and unacceptable behaviour; some are abandoned to a life of drugs or vice which rapidly leads to crime. A few recent stories from newspapers illustrate the scale of the problem.

- A 16-year-old in Bristol was sentenced for stealing 52 cars in 11 months.
- A 10-year-old in Plymouth was found guilty of kidnapping and assaulting a four-month-old baby in Plymouth.
- A 14-year-old was found guilty of 1,000 burglaries and the theft of 100 cars.
- A 15-year-old remanded in Scarborough to a secure unit escaped outside the court. He had been arrested nearly 50 times.
- In Luton, three schoolboys robbed a building society at gunpoint during their lunch hour.
- A 17-year-old murdered an 88-year-old lady (stamping repeatedly on her chest) and beat her sister in a horrendous

spree of violent raids on at least 20 people. He had been preying on pensioners since the age of 12.

- A judge in Bedford sentenced a teenager for slashing a boy's neck and sucking out the blood.

When people like this live in your street or go to your school, it is virtually impossible to avoid some kind of contact or involvement. Everyone, from cabinet minsters' sons to children living in idyllic, rural locations, is susceptible to peer-group pressure. Life can become one long dare – and you can be cold-shouldered for not playing the game. If you do join in, you are included in 'the gang' and told that you are 'cool'. It takes real courage to say, 'That's wrong,' or 'I don't want to be involved in that.'

Fifty per cent of those found guilty of criminal offences in the United Kingdom today are under the age of 21.

The power of drugs

Drugs are one of the most dangerous influences on young people today. That is why the Government has appointed a 'Drugs Czar', specifically to wage war on the expanding and criminal industry responsible for destroying so many people's lives. The appointment was spurred on by the death of Leah Betts after taking an Ecstasy tablet, a particularly tragic example of the consequences of the systematic attempt by pushers and users to draw more and more young people into the net. Yet barely a day goes by without someone mindlessly calling for drugs to be legalized.

The news that the Home Secretary's son had sold drugs to an *agent provocatrice* no doubt gave malicious pleasure to many of those who want to see freer and easier drug availability. Once the identity of the minister and his son had been revealed, after relentless speculation, the Home Secretary was personally and politically under siege. But the mock indignation of opposition politicians is always nauseating. Predictable hand-wringing and calls for resignation merely underlined the banal nature of posturing party politics, and did nothing to further the cause of either side of the debate.

More lethal in the long term are the continuing calls for decriminalization, starting with a 'soft' drug like cannabis – which the Home Office Minister George Howarth has rightly described as irresponsible.

During the 1992–7 Parliament I was Vice Chairman of the All-Party Parliamentary Committee on Drugs Misuse (a group which aired the issues and made representations to the Minister, opposing legalization). Advocates say legal drugs would cost less: there would be fewer associated crimes to fund drug habits. This entirely misses the point. In one recent year, for example, 160 babies were born addicted to purified cocaine. Crack babies are born underweight and require detoxification. What a start in life. How will it help if cocaine is legalized?

Drugs are harmful. Making them cheaper and more easily available simply increases consumption and the damage they do. In Holland in 1976 there were 10 coffee shops selling drugs. Since decriminalization, 3,000 more have opened. Drugs use has increased as a direct result of legalization.

Drugs are harmful. Making them cheaper and more easily available simply increases consumption and the damage they do.

Nothing soft about drugs

Advocates for legalization also claim that cannabis is no more harmful than cigarettes or alcohol. But 110,000 people die from smoking-related diseases each year: it is not a persuasive argument. Animal experiments suggest that cannabis damages the brain's signalling system responsible for communication. Susan Kaplin, Research Officer for Drugs Watch International, says there are more than 10,000 medical studies documenting the harmful effects of cannabis: 'It adversely affects the respiratory, cardio-vascular and immune systems. There are more than 420 chemicals in cannabis and many of these are toxic. The amounts of some cancer-causing chemicals in cannabis smoke are 50–70% greater than in tobacco smoke.'[2]

Other statistics on drugs use are equally disturbing.

- The Home Office estimates that 1.5 million people in the UK use cannabis.
- Another 20,000 are registered drug addicts.
- In one recent year 14 people died after taking Ecstasy.
- There are now an estimated 500,000 regular users of Ecstasy in the UK – almost all are young people.
- The Henley Centre has estimated that more than 1 million young people attend rave parties each week, at which Ecstasy, speed, cannabis and other drugs are available.
- A Merseyside survey suggests that one in 25 people aged 15–30 have tried hard drugs at least once.
- Manchester University say that in one recent year 47 per cent of the region's adolescents tried an illicit drug.
- In the same year 71 per cent of the region's young people had been in situations where drugs had been offered to them.

Teenagers already spend an average of £14 per week on alcohol according to a TSB survey of 2,700 14–17-year-olds. The Health Education Survey (1989) revealed that 20 per cent of first-time smokers are under 10 years of age. Is there any evidence to suggest that the response to legalized cannabis would be any different? Demand would rise exponentially, not only requiring significant sums of money, but also leaving the user damaged.

There is nothing soft about any drugs – they leave a trail of hurt and unfocused people in their wake.

It takes a strong and confident young person to resist and say 'no' when drugs are offered at a party and everyone else seems to be saying 'yes'. Drugs are often given out free in the first instance in order to cultivate an appetite and then a craving. Youngsters are encouraged to develop a taste for so-called soft drugs, such as cannabis, which then becomes the first step towards a drug-dependent life. There is nothing soft about any drugs – they leave a trail of hurt and unfocused people in their wake.

Lack of hope, lack of love

Drugs respect no barriers of class or background and they are readily available on the streets and in schools throughout the country.

The lack of hope and expectation – and often a lack of love – in the lives of many young people combines with society's failure to properly promote their emotional, mental, educational and physical welfare. The result is a loss of motivation, self-respect and self-confidence.

Into this spiritual and emotional vacuum step the drugs pushers, exploiting the young people's longing to escape from the harsh realities of abandonment and more than happy to separate them from their money. As the money runs out, the young people start to steal – first from their families and then from anybody in order to feed the addiction. In one recent year in Greater Manchester, 50 per cent of the 300,000 criminal incidents which occurred were drug related.

The real way forward will be found in restoring a sense of hope in young people.

The way out

Rather than revelling pointlessly in the misfortune of a high-profile family, we would do better to renew our determination to persuade young people to choose a drugs-free lifestyle – a lifestyle free of dependence on dangerous substances and on those who manipulate the users. The Home Office could make a start by using every penny of the seized assets of drugs barons to help addicts and to fund prevention and education measures. This would be a tangible way of demonstrating that crime does not pay as well as helping individual victims and drug-infested communities.

The real way forward, however, will be found in restoring a sense of hope in young people.

- Part of the problem is spiritual. Drugs fill a spiritual void: surely we can work to fill the void with more positive things.

- Part of the problem is the loss of self-confidence which leads people to undervalue themselves and try to compensate for this through drugs. In our schools, homes and local communities we need to find ways of affirming each person's unique worth.

- The same lack of confidence leads them to conform to a drugs culture where 'everybody does it', and where it seems impossible to say 'no'. Children and young people must be encouraged to think for themselves and not simply follow the crowd.

- Part of the problem concerns the future. Young people need to know that they are valued and that there will be a worthwhile contribution for them to make in tomorrow's world.

In Liverpool I have been greatly impressed by one group, Dare To Care, established in the Toxteth area. Undertaking support work and education, they expose the drugs culture for the sham that it is. They also have a practical and compassionate approach to helping addicts beat their addiction. More rehabilitation centres are needed in Britain and lessons should be learnt from some of the success stories – which often involve former drug users who have had the confidence to beat their addiction and then put their own experience at the service of others.

Other influences at work

Greater concern should also be shown for other negative or destructive influences at work in young people's lives.

- 64,000 children are in local authority care with broken homes behind them.
- 800,000 British children have no contact with their fathers.
- Over a period of seven years Childline counselled 343,000 children.
- 10,000 children telephone Childline for help *every day*.
- Nearly 100,000 young people go missing in Britain each year.
- 68,000 16- and 17-year-olds in the UK are not in education and have been, or still are, without a training place or a job.
- The Family Policy Studies Centre estimates that as many as one in five 21-year-olds are innumerate and one in seven illiterate.

If young people are untrained, unemployed or homeless, they risk becoming permanent drifters dangerously cut off from the rest of society. At the very least they are going to feel let down by those around them, with damaged confidence about their own worth and place in the community.

Is it any wonder that these young people often become a source of social unrest and crime? A Liverpool youth worker told me that each year about 3 per cent of local young people are excluded from school and that they are the ones who carry out most of the crime in the area. The obvious links between crime and exclusion from school, broken homes and illiteracy should lead us to think of better remedies than blanket curfews on young people.

Young people are getting badly messed up. If we are not filling them with drugs, robbing them of security, or denying them hope in a worthwhile future, we are leaving them to the tender mercies of the video and virtual reality industry. What hope of escaping the net has any youngster lacking in confidence or lacking the support of people around them ready to encourage them to resist the pull of popular culture? We sap their confidence and fill their minds with destructive material and then express horror at the consequences.

---

*Young people are getting badly messed up. If we are
not filling them with drugs, robbing them of security,
or denying them hope in a worthwhile future, we are
leaving them to the tender mercies of the video
and virtual reality industry.*

Lies, damned lies and government reports

Disraeli once rubbished some statistics which did not suit his argument with his much quoted aphorism that there are 'lies, damned lies and statistics'. He might have said the same about academic reports produced for government departments. At the beginning of 1998 a Home Office report appeared which was widely described as 'proving' that violent videos do *not* lead those who watch them to crime. In fact, that was not exactly what the report said, but its findings turned out to be easily manipulated.

The report came from Birmingham University and compared the reactions of 122 males aged between 15 and 21. They were divided into three groups: 54 violent offenders, 28 non-violent offenders, and a control sample of 40 non-offenders (school and college students). The study examined four areas:

1. Do violent young offenders view video films more often than the other two groups?
2. Do they identify more often with violent scenes and characteristics?
3. Do they remember more from violent videos?
4. Do they have more violent childhood experiences that influence their video preferences?

Essentially, the report's answer to all four questions was 'yes'.

With a suitable academic ambiguity, the report states in its conclusions that 'when factors associated with offending are present a preference for violent films and characters can distinguish offenders'.

Sometimes, maybe, perhaps. The report's writers are at pains to point out that the research cannot prove one way or another whether video violence *causes* crime. But of course no one ever said that it could; no one ever said that violent videos *alone* are the only cause of real-life violence in our communities. But if they contribute to the problem, surely this should be honestly recognized and some action taken – if nothing else to protect young people from yet another destructive influence on their lives?

Distorted perceptions

Controlled leaks of the report – presumably by those who want to see uncontrolled viewing of violent material – set the climate for how the report was covered by the press. Buried in the small print of the official Home Office press release responding to the report were the words: 'Violent films may reinforce distorted perceptions about appropriate means of resolving conflict and responding to provocation.' Quite so.

Children imitate what they see.

Other investigations have been more definite about their discoveries. Professor Elizabeth Newsome, and nearly 30 of the country's leading child psychologists, psychiatrists and paediatricians, were nearer the mark when they said they had previously been 'naive' in underestimating the link between what children see and how they behave. In Sweden, Professor Inga Soneson of the University of Lund followed the development of 200 children in Malmö, southern Sweden, aged 6–16. The study showed that in all, 14 per cent of the children who watched more than two hours' television a day at six were rated as being much more aggressive than their classmates by fifth grade (10–11 years). In the eighth grade (13–14) these children were the most aggressive in their class and watched considerably more video violence than their classmates.

Film-maker David Puttnam asked in a letter to me, 'What proof are we looking for? Does the railway company wait for someone to be killed by a train before fencing off the railway line?'

Just before Christmas 1997, 27,000 people sent a petition to Parliament calling for tighter controls. The common sense of parents – which well understands that children imitate what they see – is often the best yardstick of all.

Destructive entertainment

In our homes virtual reality allows us to kill, maim, brutalize or abuse one another through video games or computer software without any 'real' consequences. Near-real worlds are more comfortable than the hard realities of life; true values invariably become casualties – in both worlds.

In one average week on British television more than 400 killings are screened, along with 119 woundings and 27 sex attacks on women. Vicious weapons are wielded, abusive language is the norm. All of this is bizarrely described as 'entertainment'. Is it any wonder that we become emotionally deadened and come to see violence as acceptable? James Ferman, Director of the British Board of Film Classification, said: 'Children will imitate anything they see. If destruction is made to look like fun then kids will copy.'[3] What a pity, then, that his Board has not grasped the opportunity to protect young people and to do everything they can to reverse these trends.

Images imprinted in childhood often remain in the mind of the adult.

Confident citizens need to challenge this culture of violence as entertainment – first in their own homes and lives and then on a wider scale. Young minds are highly impressionable and the images imprinted in childhood often remain in the mind of the adult. They deserve protection. Confident citizens, keeping firm hold of the true values in the real world, will recognize virtual reality for the great deception which it undoubtedly is, and will protect their homes from being dominated by it.

- Avoid putting televisions and video recorders in children's bedrooms.

- Find other things for the family to do together rather than always slumping in front of the television.
- Take steps to stop pornographic material entering the home via the Internet.
- Discuss with young people the violent nature of much popular culture – have they actually thought about its possible consequences?
- Show them how to challenge the programme makers: they produce whatever they think will draw the biggest audience, so pressure can be brought to bear by nothing more demanding than switching off or refusing to buy.

Other dragons

Confident citizens need to slay any number of dragons to rescue society from the overwhelming pressures which threaten it. Once they have seen off the drug pushers and the manipulators seeking to control their minds, they will want to turn their attention to other presumptions of the new orthodoxy – upside-down assumptions on everything from personal manners to the sanctity of human life. There are dangerous and insidiously destructive forces at work, undermining long-held and precious values.

A few years ago I received a letter from a Bradford mother, Jenny Bacon, whose 14-year-old daughter, Caroline, had been prescribed the contraceptive drug Femodene ED. This was initially without the knowledge of her mother, who believes that the drug caused Caroline's death.

Mrs Bacon discovered that the Edmund Street Family Planning Clinic in Bradford had prescribed the drug and she telephoned the clinic to protest, not realizing that a 14-year-old could be given the pill without parental consent.

Within six months Caroline was suffering from headaches, flashing lights in her vision, numbness on the side of her face and paraesthesia in her hands – symptoms which the doctors assured Mrs Bacon would soon pass. But the symptoms worsened. Caroline had a fit and went into a coma. When she came round two weeks later, all she could move were her eyes. Her family were at her bedside to the end. At the inquest, a verdict of natural causes was recorded.

Public policy safeguards the clinics and the companies – who is safeguarding the young girls?

A spokesman for Schering Health Care, the manufacturer of Femodene ED, said that the pill always carried a slight risk, but that it was a doctor's right to prescribe it for girls under 16. Public policy safeguards the clinics and the companies – and their lucrative profits. Each year more than 50,000 girls under the age of 16 are prescribed the pill by clinics. Who is safeguarding the young girls?

Challenging presumptions

Confident citizens need to challenge presumptions which lead to contempt for parents and a lack of proper care for the effects on young people, and which merely generate profits for the pharmaceutical companies. Young people who challenge the cynical presumptions of the clinics need our admiration and encouragement.

Those who say they know best argue that more easily available contraceptive pills reduce teenage pregnancy, abortions and sexually transmitted diseases. After 30 years of this approach – with the pill in ready supply, along with the never-ending mantra 'if it feels good, do it' – its supporters emerge as the sowers of personal confusion, not confidence.

- In the USA gonorrhoea has become the most commonly reported disease in school-age children – surpassing measles, mumps, chicken pox and rubella combined.
- 2.5 million teenagers in the USA suffer from a sexually transmitted disease.
- 40 per cent of pregnancies in the under-19 age group in the USA are aborted and 60 per cent of those girls are under 15.
- In the UK new cases of sexually transmitted diseases have trebled since 1976.
- One in five British pregnancies ends in abortion – 5 million in 30 years.

- 24 out of 30 pieces of published research cite a direct link between abortion and breast cancer.

The confident citizen will demand to know all the facts about sexually transmitted diseases, the side-effects of the pill, the dangers of infertility after abortion, and AIDS. The confident citizen will want to know about post-abortion syndrome, the pain her unborn child will feel, and how some pre-natal tests can kill the baby. The confident citizen will not be bamboozled into blind conformity. There are alternatives to abortion (adoption, for example). How often are these alternatives mentioned as possibilities? How often are pressurized young women, who may feel they have 'no choice', offered space to think and constructive help?

I once met a teenage woman who had taken refuge in a Life House on the south coast. Her father had flown into a rage when he learned that she was pregnant and had thrown her out of their home. A few weeks later, he came to ask her forgiveness and welcomed her and her unborn child – his grandchild – back home. If that Life House had not been there for her, offering support in the hopeless weeks before her father took her back home, she would almost certainly have aborted the child and given into the pressure of social workers and doctors, who told her she would not be able to cope.

How often are pressurized young women, who may feel they have 'no choice', offered space to think and constructive help?

We can do much, much more to provide practical help for young women in this kind of situation. Judgementalism and condemnation will get us nowhere: everyone makes mistakes. The issue is what we do about them. Our instincts tell us that destructive remedies rarely produce long-term positive outcomes. More creative solutions must surely be based on unconditional love and practical support for a mother and her child. One important step would certainly be for more of the men involved to have the confidence to accept their responsibility, rather than simply standing back while their girlfriend and child are subjected to the abortionist's knife.

Just say 'no'

When Anita, a single Liverpool woman in her twenties, became pregnant, a scan revealed a chink in her baby's leg. She declined the abortion she was offered, amazed that such a minor cosmetic disability was a legal ground for abortion.

After her next scan, she was told that the child would suffer from dwarfism. She again declined the abortion.

On the third occasion, she was told the baby was growing again but would be multiply handicapped.

Following her third refusal to abort the child, a social worker arrived at her mother's home and told her mother that a bed had been booked for Anita at the local hospital for the following Monday. The hospital and social workers had decided that a single young woman would never be able to bring up a severely disabled baby.

Anita had the confidence and the determination to say 'no' once again. It took real courage to act against the forceful 'advice' of the medical staff, and instead of being a time of happiness and joy her pregnancy became a nightmare.

There was nothing wrong with baby Lauren when she was born and the child's father, Terry Anderson, supported Anita throughout and subsequently married her. Anita had gone through three separate tests, which had all pointed to varying degrees of disability in the baby. All the tests had been wrong, but no doctor or social worker ever apologized to Anita Anderson for the misery which they had caused her. Her courage in standing up to the medical establishment and the social workers, and against a raw prejudice towards disabled people, is admirable. Anita and Terry knew what they believed to be the right course of action: they were prepared to love their child whether she was handicapped or not, and were confident enough to stick to their guns despite the pressures to do otherwise.

She risked her whole future to stand up and say 'no'
when something went against her principles.
That is a confident citizen.

Emilia Klepacka is another person who stood up for what she believed. Aged 14 and at a school in Stevenage, she learnt that the local Labour party candidate, Barbara Follett (now the MP) had been invited to distribute the school prizes. Mrs Follett is a founder member of EMILY's List – the organization which supports women parliamentary candidates, on the condition that they pledge themselves to support abortion. Emilia regarded the financing of candidates in return for such an undertaking as blood money. She was suspended from school for boycotting the school prize-giving and publicly explaining her reasons for doing so. Although subsequently reinstated, she risked her whole future to stand up and say 'no' when something went against her principles. That is a confident citizen.

Paying a price

There are others in recent years who have also stood up for what they believe – and who have paid a price for refusing to give in to all the pressures of the prevailing culture. These are just a few examples related to the abortion question:

- The scientist Michael Clark was sacked because he refused to monitor (i.e. test emission samples from) the chimney stack in Manchester where they incinerated aborted babies.
- Barbara Janaway, a medical secretary, was sacked by Salford Health Authority because she would not administer abortion applications.
- Patrick McCrystal, a pharmacist in Belfast, was sacked because he would not dispense the abortifacient morning-after pill.
- Simon Caldwell, a young journalist, lost his job at the *Wigan Evening Post* after he refused to rewrite an abortion story in 'politically correct' language.

There are countless others who have been willing to pay a price for the sake of sticking to a strongly held principle. Liberal authoritarianism (the imposition of modern utilitarianism, or what is believed to be the greatest good for the greatest number) isolates, excludes and demonizes anyone who rejects its sacred cows. Its exponents, from the media, politics, professions and judiciary, use all the techniques at their disposal – manipulated government reports, loaded committees of enquiry devoid of opposition, and a propaganda machine worthy of a police state – to create and manipulate public opinion.

Speaking out may cost something, but why should we sit back and let the 'authorities' tell us what to think? They do not necessarily know best.

Confident citizens need their wits about them to withstand this constant assault. In particular they should challenge the composition of the many committees established to consider ethical issues. Their findings can have a huge long-term effect on legislation, covering as they do issues as diverse as genetics, cloning, embryology, the legalization of drugs, and the effect of broadcasting gratuitous violence. Time and again a tame philosopher (often the same person) is asked to chair a committee. The committee is carefully handpicked and the report's conclusions can be confidently predicted even before the committee has met. This sham is dressed up as a public consultation, but in reality it is cynicism worthy of a one-party state.

We could all do more to challenge this state of affairs, and get involved with demanding more genuine, open discussions on these vital questions. Speaking out may cost something, but why should we sit back and let the 'authorities' tell us what to think, or what is right and wrong? They do not necessarily know best.

The next test: death

While the abortion debate has been running for a long time now, the next great test of nerve centres on our attitudes towards the sick and the dying. A carefully orchestrated campaign to change the law is now under way. Well organized and well financed supporters of euthanasia are systematically pursuing their objectives in our courts and medical institutions, through Parliament and through the media. In deploying a battery of highly paid lawyers, lobbyists and 'hard cases', they are following the textbook approach which was first deployed, to devastating effect, in 1967 when the laws on abortion were changed.

Thirty years ago public opinion on abortion was first softened up by a series of lurid and tragic cases. If ever proof was needed of the old juridical saying that 'hard cases make bad law', surely the 1967 Abortion Act provides it. Parliament was assured that legalized abortion would not lead to a general right to kill the unborn; that it was not a slippery slope. Five million abortions later – with the accompanying horrors of destructive experiments on human embryos, human cloning and genetic manipulation – those arguments are exposed as a monstrous deceit, but it nonetheless takes real confidence to resist them: abortion as the solution to an unwanted pregnancy has become a firm part of the prevailing culture.

Hoping for similar success in manipulating public opinion and stirring up pressure for change, in 1989 the euthanasia lobby saw an opportunity to exploit the 'hard case' of Tony Bland, a Liverpool football supporter critically injured at Hillsborough, who was in a deep coma known as a persistent vegetative state. A court case was brought to obtain legal permission to end Tony's life.

The lawyer Lord Lester was appointed as *amicus curiae* – an impartial 'friend of the court', there to give objective advice – and he asserted that 'the artificial prolongation of corporeal existence' may degrade and demean humanity. He stated that life is only valuable as a vehicle for consciousness. This defines humanity and equates life with the ability to think. Insensibility becomes a fate worse than death itself and even becomes a disqualification for life.

For the first time the courts crossed the line and legally sanctioned the intentional killing of a patient: euthanasia.

This argument won the day in the Bland Judgement which was eventually reached in 1992. For the first time the courts crossed the line and legally sanctioned the intentional killing of a patient:

euthanasia. The tubes used to feed Tony Bland were removed and he starved to death. A number of law lords expressed serious reservations about the case. Lord Mustill stated that 'the withdrawal of nutrition and hydration was designed to bring about death. That was why it was done. It was decided that it was time he died.' He clearly understood that this was not simply a question of allowing someone to die, but deliberately bringing an end to their life.

It is instructive to note that another young Liverpool supporter, Andrew Devine, then a constituent of mine, was also injured at Hillsborough. Like Tony Bland, he also went into a deep coma. After eight years, Andrew became aware of his surroundings once more and was starting to communicate with his family.

We do not know, of course, whether Tony Bland would have recovered. What we do know is that a British court sanctioned his killing. This was a fearsome breach which the Law Commission is now seeking to incorporate as Statute through a Mental Incapacity Bill. Amongst others, the Church of England Board of Social Responsibility has opposed this move, because they say such awesome decisions should not be made routinely: each and every circumstance should at least be considered as a separate case.

Lethal arguments

The extension of the euthanasia argument, logical enough if you accept the basic premise, came in the medical journal *The Lancet*. A leading physician, Sir Raymond Hoffenberg, suggested that patients in a persistent vegetative state should be given lethal injections and their organs taken for transplant. So now we have it: if you become insensible we can avoid the costs and inconvenience of care and hospices, and rather than waste your mortal remains by starving you to death, you will be killed 'cleanly' and used instead as a rich source of organs.

The flaws in this argument revolve around questions of consent, the commissioning of doctors and nurses as killers, and the fundamental question of life itself. But how many people will be confident enough to stand up to the battery of commentators, lawyers, propagandists and hard cases being used to undermine the widespread opposition to the deliberate killing of patients?

> *How many people will be confident enough to stand up to the battery of commentators, lawyers, propagandists and hard cases being used to undermine the widespread opposition to the deliberate killing of patients?*

The present law recognizes a clear distinction between killing and letting die. 'Care' and 'kill' cannot be used as synonyms. But are we confident enough in ourselves to defend this line against those who are attacking it – or will we abandon these defences and retreat once again?

In 1997 Lord Lester, no longer an impartial adviser, went to the High Court on another case. He tried to obtain a legal ruling to allow the doctor of Annie Lindsell – who suffered from motor neurone disease – to administer drugs which would relieve her mental and physical distress during the final stages of the disease, but which would also shorten life. The case was financed by the Voluntary Euthanasia Society. It collapsed because it was agreed that under the principle of 'double effect' no court ruling was needed. If a doctor's motive is control of pain, the treatment is always acceptable, even if the drugs used accelerate death as a side effect. If, however, the doctor's primary motive is deliberately to accelerate death, it is criminal. The euthanasia propagandists were not going to make the progress they hoped for with this show case.

Dangerous philosophers

Yet, inevitably, luminaries such as Baroness Warnock were on hand to tell us that the law did need to be 'clarified' and that this was not a 'slippery slope'. G.K. Chesterton once wrote that 'the most dangerous criminal now is the lawless modern philosopher'.[4] He had a point. Why should we accept that the law needs to be clarified when we know that clarification will be a cover for all manner of dangerous excesses?

> *'No one need die in agony. It is not necessary to legalize mercy killing/euthanasia to make this claim a reality.'*

David Oliver, Medical Director of Wisdom Hospice said: 'I am mystified why Ms Lindsell and Dr Holmes felt it necessary to go to court over a treatment that is readily available to her in the first place, and which doctors carry out daily without fear of prosecution.'

Dr Robert Twycross, Macmillan Clinical Reader in Palliative Medicine at the University of Oxford, said: 'No one need die in agony. It is not necessary to legalize mercy killing/euthanasia to make this claim a reality.'

Lord Williams of Mostyn, speaking for the Government, said the present law was not 'difficult or obscure'. The Bishop of Southwell, speaking for Anglican and Catholic bishops, said they would be 'resolutely opposed to the legalisation of euthanasia'. Lord McColl, for the Conservatives, said: 'Those in favour of euthanasia are deliberately seeking to change our statute law by causing confusion and public anxiety and by discrediting the current legal framework.' Yet the campaign goes on.

Collapsed court cases which uphold the existing law – and lawyers fees – do not come cheap. The VES say the Annie Lindsell case cost them £50,000. Extraordinarily, out of the jaws of defeat, Lord Lester claimed in the press: 'We won what we wanted.' What is it that the VES want?

Routine killing

Dr Michael Irwin, Chairman of the VES, was pictured in the summer of 1997 holding a 'customized exit bag' (used for the disposal of dead bodies) and claiming to have helped 50 people to die. He told the *Daily Telegraph*: 'I do not believe I can be convicted.'

> *The legalized killing of patients will fundamentally alter their relationship with their doctor.*

The VES will not be satisfied until the killing of terminally ill patients becomes an integral and routine part of every doctor's job. Through ad hoc legal rulings and by using the proposed Law Commission's Bill on Mental Incapacity (rejected by the last Government) as a Trojan horse, they hope we will drift into legalized euthanasia by default. What will the consequences be?

The legalized killing of patients will fundamentally alter their relationship with their doctor. Not only might patients grow to fear their physicians, but other abuses will also creep in. In Holland, where voluntary euthanasia is legal, the Remmelink Commission established in 1990 by the Dutch Attorney General found that in one recent year, out of a total of 3,300 euthanasia deaths, 1,030 had not been specifically requested by the patient. Compulsion and pressure are apparently not very far behind 'voluntary' euthanasia. Is that really what we want?

Positive action for life

As the British Medical Association has strongly asserted, euthanasia is morally, legally and medically unacceptable. Parliament should ensure that it stays that way. On past performance no one should hold their breath – certainly not until more confident citizens emerge ready to say 'no'.

The danger is already clear. Public opinion is being softened up by a string of hard cases which play on pain and suffering. Anyone who opposes the routine incorporation of euthanasia will be mocked and criticized for being 'in favour of pain', or 'in favour of suffering'. Eventually, Dutch-style laws will undoubtedly be brought in for Britain – unless the alternative view is clearly and confidently put forward, upholding the sanctity of human life, the traditional values of the Hippocratic Oath, and the importance of hospice provision (where so much is known now about controlling pain in terminally ill patients).

We can all take positive and practical action by informing ourselves about the ethical and legal issues, lobbying our politicians, and making certain that our local hospices receive all the help they need.

Essential Questions

- How would you teach children to stand up to bullies at school?
- How do you think children can be prepared to resist the temptation of crime?
- Do you understand what factors can cause violent behaviour and crime?
- What more do you think might be done to counteract these factors with more positive influences?
- Are you confident about saying 'no' to something you believe is wrong?
- Is enough being done to counter the arguments in favour of the legalization of drugs or euthanasia? Do you think there is anything you can do as an individual?
- Are there local support groups for drug addicts or women with unplanned/unwanted pregnancies, or a hospice where you could lend your support?
- How would you react if a doctor or social worker counselled the abortion of your baby on grounds of disability?
- Have you ever stood up for a principle despite the risk to a friendship or job? If not, would you be prepared to do so?

5/ Citizen Action

In January 1998 Martin Bell MP gave one of the Roscoe Lectures on Good Citizenship run by Liverpool John Moores University. The former BBC war correspondent's defeat of Neil Hamilton at Tatton in the 1997 General Election vividly symbolized the electorate's dismay at the whole 'cash for questions' row which had been dogging politics for some time. John Major once rightly complained that the House of Commons had become a hiring fair.

Martin Bell's victory was symbolic for another reason, too. It represented the ability of the electorate – what Bell tends to call 'the little people' – to determine the shape of events. At the declaration of his election victory, Bell recalled the words of G.K. Chesterton from his famous poem of 1915, 'The Secret People':

Smile at us, pay us, pass us; but do not quite forget.
For we are the people of England, that never have spoken yet.

The 'secret people' can, from time to time, stage at least a minor insurrection against their leaders, who should never take them for granted. That is what happened at Tatton.

A woman who lives in the Liverpool district of Toxteth put a question to Martin Bell at the end of his Roscoe Lecture. She asked what she, personally, could do about politics. How could she be active, without necessarily joining a political party, none of which attracted her? How can ordinary people understand how the political system works and influence the way their society, their community is run? In this chapter I want to look at what is involved in political activism.

A good place to start

It is often strong feelings on a particular issue which prompts people to become politically active. Take the housing problem, for example. On 4 May 1972, the counting of votes for Liverpool's Low Hill Ward took place at the City's St George's Hall. Against all the odds a 21-year-old student was elected. I had decided to stand in that ward because the party politicians had determined to demolish people's homes, after having neglected them for years on end. Half the homes had no inside sanitation and many of the streets were still lit by gas lamps – yet it was not too late for improvement and renewal rather than destruction.

How can ordinary people understand how the political system works and influence the way their society, their community is run?

The recent debate about using Green Belt land to build 5 million new homes reminds me of that period. The policy – which I have attacked in the House of Lords – is just as badly thought out, and is just the sort of muddle-headed policy which could be successfully challenged if local people got involved, got informed and started arguing. A close look at the overall housing situation today should be enough to encourage worried citizens out of their armchairs.

- We need more properties, but not because there are more people. Generally more people are living alone – and more than 40 per cent of families now break up, so two properties are needed instead of one.

- There are 800,000 empty homes in England alone – 8,000 just in the city of Liverpool.

- There is no shortage of Brown Field sites (derelict sites in urban areas), but rather than rebuild on these, renovate empty homes and breathe new life into the cities, the politicians go for the easy option of demolition every time. This waste is then compounded by the destruction of our few remaining open spaces and tracts of countryside to make way for new houses.

- Many houses are under-occupied, particularly by the elderly, reducing resources for family accommodation. But elderly people are understandably reluctant to move from a much-loved home if the only alternatives are inaccessible high-rise flats, properties away from familiar areas and relatives, or institutional 'homes'. There are simply not enough more positive choices, such as granny flats, annexes on family homes and sheltered accommodation offering security and independence.

I quote this example because it is where I began in elected politics and it shows how politicians are still addressing symptoms not causes. It brings quicker, more tangible results, which is attractive when you have elections to win. No one ever really asks the 'little people' what they think. Why not take the initiative and speak out? You will probably find that others agree with you; all it takes is one confident person to speak their mind, and a pressure campaign on those making the decisions is under way.

Back in 1972, I gave the voters a blank piece of paper and told them that, as politicians' promises were largely worthless, and as I could not afford to print glossy election leaflets, I would like them to give their own views on the Council's proposals for their community and put these in the ballot box with their voting papers. Hundreds did and many voted for me at the same time.

A few years later, as the City Council's new Housing Committee Chairman, and as the Council's Deputy Leader, I was able to announce the biggest housing renewal programme in the country and to declare that we were 'pensioning off the bulldozer'.

Election apathy

For me it was a good introduction to the effectiveness of political activism. Individual efforts do pay off. Not many people seem to believe that at the moment, however, and this is particularly obvious where voting is concerned. The biggest foe in my first election, and every subsequent election which I contested, was not my opponents but apathy and disillusionment with politics and politicians on the part of the electorate. 'You're all the same; whoever gets in, nothing changes,' was a familiar charge. 'None of you listen to what we think,' was another. I countered these remarks by reminding people that doing nothing never changes anything. Gradually I was rewarded by seeing election turnouts increase. Voters repay loyalty towards them with loyalty to the politician who clearly puts their interests first. If people knew you had helped them or their families, they were prepared to accept that you might not be in politics just for personal gain or aggrandizement, and that maybe it was worth voting after all.

Doing nothing never changes anything.

One of the most depressing things about Liverpool politics in recent years – and it is the same in other areas of poverty and deprivation – has been the inability of politicians to inspire the voters to cast their votes.

- In one constituency in the 1997 General Election nearly half the voters just stayed at home.
- In the May 1996 local elections just 27.3 per cent – less than one in three – voted.
- In a December 1997 council by-election in the Melrose Ward, the turnout plummeted to 6.2 per cent – possibly an all-time UK low.
- In May 1998 turnout for local elections in Liverpool stood at 22 per cent, with almost four out of five of the city's voters declining to vote.

If the electorate are saying so clearly that they are completely disillusioned with party politics and with our whole political system, then all who care for our civic life should urgently consider ways of bringing local democracy back to life. The consequences could be catastrophic if this does not happen.

- Disinclination to vote, reluctance to participate in community and countrywide matters, increasing alienation from all levels of government and widespread cynicism will badly undermine our democratic institutions.

- No politician can possibly claim a democratic mandate when so few voters take part in the process.

- Such widespread rejection or lack of interest in democracy will be a fertile breeding ground for anti-democratic organizations and ideologies.

How has this negative situation come about? Is there a way to repair the damage and restore people's faith in political life and enthusiasm for community action?

Why disillusionment has set in

Politicians often seem blissfully – or culpably – unaware of the low esteem in which they are held by the public.

For the best part of two years in the mid-1990s I served on Parliament's senior committee, the Committee of Privileges, investigating what was popularly known as 'cash for questions'. It was not merely the individual acts of dishonesty which exercised me, but also the disgust which was being directed at all politicians because of it. The culture of lobbying and serving commercial interests for financial gain had become deeply entrenched among members of the House of Commons. It had undermined the concepts of public service and public duty.

In an article in the *Guardian* newspaper, I warned that in the end the politicians are only as good as the people who elect them. It all depends on our own willingness to be active citizens. Democracies get the politicians they deserve and the ethics which they vote for.[1] If we do not bother to find out about a politician's business interests or beliefs, we have little right to complain later when we discover that our MP has commercial activities which clash with his or her political duties, or is voting for measures with which we profoundly disagree.

Armchair activism

But how active are we prepared to be if something is happening which we do not like? Talking is always easy, of course. The armchair activist sits at home complaining but not doing anything constructive. We are all guilty of this at times – but in reality there are any number of actions we could take. Residents' associations, tenants' groups, single issue campaigns, trades unions, professional associations, political parties, voluntary organizations and charity work are all there for us to take part in. We can make a difference, but not by sitting at home.

The tendency to talk rather than act can easily rear its head again even when we do decide to get involved. Beware the terrible meetings trap: good intentions often end in talking shops, from local associations to parliamentary committees. In the 1970s management trainees were shown a film entitled 'Meetings, Bloody Meetings'. John Cleese magnificently parodied the ineffectual and relentless rounds of meetings into which we are so easily sucked. Politicians often wrongly assume that membership of committees and attendance at endless meetings equals effective activity.

'God so loved the world, he didn't send a committee.'

In politics, the meeting is an occupational hazard – and an extremely easy way to claim that some important question is being properly addressed. Often it is simply an excuse for obfuscation rather than action.

The more controversial the question, the grander the committee. In liberal circles (mainly elitist figures pursuing a rights-based agenda) you simply call for the setting up of a Royal Commission if you want to dodge having to take a view. Recently there have been calls for Royal Commissions on the legalization of drugs and euthanasia. To counter this unerring political instinct for avoiding direct decision-making, I now keep a poster on my office wall to remind me that 'God so loved the world, he didn't send a committee'.

A matter of privilege

The Committee of Privileges is about as self-important and as grand as parliamentary committees can get. During its enquiry into cash for questions, it insisted – against my wishes and those of a sizeable minority – on holding its proceedings 'in camera', excluding the press and public. At the end of its deliberations in 1997 the Committee passed its papers to Sir Gordon Downey, the Parliamentary Commissioner for Standards, whose post had been created in the wake of Lord Nolan's 1996 report into standards in public life.

The Committee handed over its papers to Sir Gordon, having declared itself incompetent – a word with a deliciously broad variety of interpretations – to investigate the range of allegations which had been laid before it during the previous two years.

While the Committee huffed and puffed over little matters, the central questions concerning a compromised political system were being wilfully ignored.

An obsession with trivia occupied most of the Committee's time. But while the Committee huffed and puffed over little matters, the central questions concerning a compromised political system were being wilfully ignored. Cynics might wonder whether those who manage these things – 'the usual channels' (the whips), the spin doctors and government managers – simply kept us busy with the trivia as an exercise in distraction. Certainly, whenever the more crucial issues surfaced, it proved remarkably convenient for the authorities to hide behind the cover of the Committee's never-ending deliberations. It is a prime example of the inertia which committees can generate. Some Members may have had their reasons for not wishing to reach the essential issues, and evidence did emerge that government whips had tried to exert undue influence on the proceedings.

The day of reckoning

I dissented – as a minority of one – from the Committee's final report. The Committee had failed to lay to rest the ghost of improper financial involvement, and the haphazard enquiry had to be resumed after the 1997 General Election. Failure to bring some of the principal accusers, such as Mohamed Al Fayed, back before the Committee led to central questions remaining unresolved – and left some of those who had been accused complaining that they had been unfairly treated. In turn, this led to the resignation from the Committee of Ann Widdecombe MP because she said it had not discharged its duty properly.

None of us in politics belongs to the communion of saints, but the public has a right to expect its MPs to deliver a system which guarantees financial rectitude and transparency. The extraordinary thing is that even after Lord Nolan's report and those endless committee hearings, we are still a long way from re-establishing public confidence – although the public did at least have some sort of day of reckoning on 1 May 1997.

The public has a right to expect its MPs to deliver a system which guarantees financial rectitude and transparency.

In the light of the uproar over a £1 million donation to the Labour Party by Formula 1 boss Bernie Ecclestone, and the controversy over huge overseas donations to the Conservative Party from a Chinese donor allegedly involved in drugs trafficking, the issue of political funding must remain firmly on the agenda. I, for one, am convinced that overseas donations should be banned and that an upper limit should be put on both donations and party expenditure. The 1997 General Election cost the two principal parties nearly £40 million. And advertising codes, requiring a modicum of truth, do not apply when politicians are spending their money on billboards carrying election advertisements. This all demands much tighter regulation.

Labour must take care lest the biter is bitten. Even in the short time since the 1997 Election, the outcry over investments in off-shore trusts by Geoffrey Robinson, the Paymaster General; the sacking of a civil servant by the Foreign Secretary, Robin Cook, while he considered appointing a close friend whom he later married in her place; the Formula 1 controversy, all demonstrate Labour's susceptibility to the same temptations which ensnared the Conservatives.

The motivation behind our sleazy state is as old as the hills: the pursuit of power, personal aggrandizement, and the protection of privileges. It is not entirely coincidental and certainly not meant as irony that the watchdog charged with the job of acting as Parliament's policeman calls itself the Committee of Privileges. Too often governments protect their own privileges and live by the maxim, 'Don't do as I do, do as I say.'

As I have argued elsewhere in this book, we have passed through a decade in which unbridled individualism has been matched by the encouragement of rapacious competitiveness as good business practice. It was bound to affect our way of conducting politics.

No such thing as society

False liberalism argues that there is no such thing as society, only individuals. But authentic liberalism, ethical liberalism, knows otherwise. Ethical liberals know that freedom can only flourish within the framework of order and that their most urgent task is to rescue political liberalism and the reputation of our political system, which has been so badly tarnished by uncontrolled avarice and self-interest.

Striving for the common good should be the basis of our politics and our motive for entering political life.

In 1911 Leonard Hobhouse (one of the foremost political thinkers in Edwardian Britain), in his defining essay on 'Liberalism', said: 'Society consists wholly of persons ... The British nation is not a mysterious entity over the forty millions of living souls who dwell together under a common law. It's their life, its well-being or ill-fortune their well-being or ill-fortune. Thus, the common good to which each man's rights are subordinate is a good in which each man has a share.'[2] Writing in 1945, the French philosopher and father of European Christian Democracy Jacques Maritain insisted that 'a common action will bring forth common fruits'.[3]

Striving for the common good should be the basis of our politics and our motive for entering political life.

Unbridled individualism

Instead of the common good, however, successive governments have promoted individualism and competitiveness. Instead of public service, the clarion call has been the accumulation of wealth. The values of the financial jungle have become the civic values of our time.

The real tragedy is that many politicians do not regard such amorality as corrupt. Overhearing House of Commons tea-room conversations during the 'cash for questions' investigation, I was struck by the fact that some MPs were expressing genuine puzzlement that the public were making such a fuss. It is therefore hardly surprising that prior to the 1997 General Election they had no real concept of the extent of public cynicism.

Tolerance of a corrupt system and false liberalism are the greatest dangers we face. As public cynicism reaches a new pitch, there are hopeful signs at last of a fresh civic reckoning. Change is in the air, and here lies the opportunity for the idealist, for the active citizen. What are the areas most urgently in need of change? Where should pressure for fresh thinking be applied? There are several issues which seem to be causing the most concern.

The values of the financial jungle have become the civic values of our time.

The corruption of politics

The first thing to understand is that the corruption of our politics can take many forms. The most insidious form of corruption is that which breaches no law but is part and parcel of the system.

Since the beginning of the twentieth century we have developed a 'partyocracy' in Britain and every political party has been guilty of seeking an ascendancy that in itself tends towards corruption. In Liberal history, for example, the days of Lloyd George's peerage salesman, Maundy Gregory, illustrate the dangers very well. Lloyd George was disarmingly frank in the way in which he sold peerages, but such transactions do not require an open sale. During the last

Conservative Government one study showed that directors of companies donating more than £500,000 to Conservative Party funds had a 50 per cent better chance of receiving an honour. Harold Wilson's resignation honours – Labour's so-called 'Lavender List' – were a model in the payment of political favours. Even Tony Blair, fresh from the hustings, hotly denouncing sleaze, and notwithstanding a 175-seat majority in the House of Commons, did not escape criticism for some of his nominees for political honours.

The quango culture

The granting of honours, however, is small beer compared to the power exercised by Government ministers in appointments to quangos. The trend to parcel out power and position to the great and the good – through bodies such as development corporations – has undermined local democracy and pulled power away from the people.

- Ministers have within their gift a total of some 40,000 appointments to quangos.
- In the last Parliament a quarter of the membership of the largest quangos were known members of the Conservative Party; many more were quieter sympathizers; a third were leading industrialists.
- Since 1993 quangos have been responsible for a fifth of total public expenditure – more than £47.1 billion.
- £24 billion of this has been transferred from locally elected bodies.

This party stranglehold on patronage, power and budgets operated in the same way when Labour was last in power, before the Conservatives took over, and there has been no indication since May 1997 that the practice will change. Recently, for example, I received a letter from a woman who had shown enormous dedication and commitment to her local hospital trust for some years. She had just been notified, in a peremptory fashion, that her services were no longer required: she had been replaced by a Labour Party appointee. The process of appointments such as this is shrouded in secrecy. Talk of more open government brings to mind Mahatma Gandhi's famously dry remark about western civilization – that it would be a very good thing.

The trend to parcel out power and position to the great and the good has undermined local democracy and pulled power away from the people.

Whose bread I eat

The merging of the interests of big corporations and political parties does not stop at the quangos: it reaches deep into Parliament itself. Figures prepared before May 1997 show that no main party is immune:

- 135 Conservative MPs held 287 directorships and 146 consultancies between them.
- 29 Labour members shared 60 directorships and 43 consultancies.
- 8 Liberal Democrats held a total of 15 such appointments.

Sir Winston Churchill once remarked that 'lobbyists are the touts of protected industries'. It is a clear case of 'whose bread I eat, his song I sing'. Yet at the very heart of our Victorian mock-Gothic pile of a Parliament in Westminster is the area known as the Central Lobby. Any democracy requires that *all* interests have lobbying access to the politicians. The issue is one of regulation and openness – and the most appropriate way of facilitating the lobbying process. How can it be kept as fair as possible?

In the mid 1980s there were over 50 major lobbying firms. One well-known lobbyist had a staff of 30 and annual earnings of over £1.8 million. A 1985 survey reported that of 180 major British companies, 41 per cent retained political consultancies for 'Government work'. Back-benchers were hired as a conduit between Government and industry.

Any democracy requires that all *interests*
have lobbying access to the politicians.

Firms do need to understand for themselves how Government and Parliament work and how best to present their case. They need to buy in well-informed briefing material from experts on governmental and parliamentary affairs, and they need, most importantly, to learn the skill of direct lobbying. In my experience the companies who used their local MPs to facilitate face-to-face meetings with ministers were likely to be better listened to than those companies who were trying to twist arms through a third party.

Elected MPs are well remunerated. Although they should not become lobbyists themselves, they may have a role in assisting companies to develop their own lobbying skills. For the purpose of fairness and openness, they – and the senior civil servants who regularly transfer to industrial posts connected with their former service to the state (to the despair of the Parliamentary Select Committees who have monitored the process and criticized it) – must properly register such interests.

Between 1975 and 1986, Enoch Powell, then MP for South Down, refused to sign the Register of Members' Interests. He did so on the delicate point that the Register had been established by a Resolution of the House of Commons when it should have been established by new Statute. He was right about the need to enact a new law, but it was merely a semantic point. More fundamentally, the Register was voluntary, it was by no means definitive of the entirety of an MP's interests, and it was secretive.

The situation has improved post-1997, although several MPs have been reprimanded since then for not fully declaring gifts and donations. In addition, the Formula 1 donation/tobacco advertising argument, or the furore over the Paymaster General's offshore interests, show that the debate is far from over. There is more work to be done. At least Parliament is now actively considering how political parties should be funded. There seems to be an emerging consensus that gifts above about £5,000 should be publicly declared.

Never in August

The most useful change which Parliament could make to encourage greater transparency would be to require all candidates at every election to list their remunerated consultancies and directorships – and then allow the electorate to make up their own minds about whether a candidate has the necessary time and detachment to attend properly to their parliamentary duties.

Once elected, MPs are now required to spell out their interests in greater detail, but far more could be done to allow the public access to the Register of Members' Interests.

You could be forgiven for thinking that they do not really want you to see the Register – especially during August when it might spoil someone's holiday.

Even post-Nolan, access to the Register is difficult.

- At Westminster a copy is kept in the Members' Library and another copy is kept in the office of the Registrar of Members' Interests.

- Every January an annual edition is published and sold by Her Majesty's Stationery Office, priced at nearly twenty pounds.

- The Register is constantly being amended, but the public may have to wait for twelve months before seeing an updated printed version.

- The only other way to see the Register is by appointment between 11.00 a.m. and 3.00 p.m., Monday to Friday – although 'during parliamentary recesses, and especially during the month of August, more limited hours of inspection apply'.

- You may then photocopy the entries – but only up to 20 pages on each of your visits made by prior appointment.

You could be forgiven for thinking that they do not really want you to see the Register – especially during August when it might spoil someone's holiday.

Where loyalty lies

Full and frank disclosure is now more likely in the wake of Lord Nolan's Standards Enquiry, despite the apparent lack of action so far, but there are still glaring anomalies.

1. *Partiality* As an elected representative, accountable primarily to your constituents, and salaried to do that job, can you also serve outside interests and those who sent you to speak for them? Human instincts, being what they are, would almost certainly draw you closer to the interests of your extra-parliamentary pay-master.

2. *Transparency* Even if it is possible to detach financial interests from political interests, can it be right for MPs to speak and vote on questions in which they have a direct, personal pecuniary interest? Following the Poulson Scandal of 1973 (in which an architect sought to influence a council leader by corrupt means), local Councillors were required to declare their interests and then to absent them-selves from debates which involved those interests. The same standards and penalties for dishonesty which go with this rule should be imposed on Parliament.

As an elected representative, accountable primarily to your constituents, and salaried to do that job, can you also serve outside interests?

I had no outside commercial interests during any of my 25 years as an elected representative. The only additional income which I received was from occasional lectures, broadcasting or writing. Although I am no longer an elected representative, I have been appointed to the Upper House. This is not salaried (although ex-penses are provided) and I am now receiving non-parliamentary income. Not only should such income be declared by all Upper House members, but the rules should be further tightened in line with the local government practice mentioned above. Where we have financial interests, we should not speak or vote.

3. *Criminality* The 1976 Royal Commission on Standards of Conduct in Public Life highlighted the loophole which prevents an MP from being subject to criminal proceedings should he or she accept a bribe: 'Neither the statutory nor the common law applies to the bribery or attempted bribery of a member of Parliament in respect of his parliamentary activities.'[4]

In 1990 the then Prime Minister, Margaret Thatcher, said that the Government would consider bringing forward legislation to make the corruption of MPs a criminal offence, 'if there was clear evidence that the present arrangements were ineffective'.[5] In the light of the enquiries into cash for questions, how much more evidence do we need?

MPs need to value their independence; they need to maximize the time needed to do the job for which they were elected; and they need to inspire confidence and respect in their honesty.

Trust and confidence undermined

There have been other downsides involved in the direct employment of MPs as parliamentary lobbyists. I recall, for example, a conversation I once had with a close parliamentary colleague. He was in the pay of a pharmaceutical giant which manufactures an abortifacient, a drug which has a proven record of damaging women's health. When he discussed initiatives I was taking against this company, on whose behalf was he questioning me? It undermined and damaged our relationship.

Of greater concern were the huge vested interests at work during the discussion of the Shops Bill and the National Lottery Bill. Those interests succeeded in buying the new parliamentary laws they wanted, but at a terrible cost. The Shops Bill, for example, has led to the loss of Sunday as a special day, 0.75 million people (mainly women) now having to work on Sundays, and all the attendant implications for their families.

I was involved in the detailed discussions on both these measures, and helped to organize the opposition. The vested interests were everywhere, constantly buying influence and favours. They were at work both outside and inside Parliament – hosting champagne receptions and dinners at party conferences, and donating significant sums of money disguised as advertisments in party publications. Some of the lobbyists were themselves parliamentary candidates who had been hired because of their knowledge of the parties. In another context it would be called insider trading.

A more open democracy – with, for instance, laws guaranteeing freedom of information – would provide better safeguards against the abuses we have seen in recent years.

Repairing trust

So what can be done to put right this drastic loss of trust in the way our country is run? Can confidence be restored in the ability of elected representatives to act for the common good rather than for vested interests? Fundamental changes must be made, and there is a need for more 'ordinary', upright citizens to become involved with the processes of local and central government.

- Lobbying and the involvement of huge outside interests must be carefully regulated and independently and openly monitored.

- They also need to be examined in the context of a secretive, overcentralized and distorted political system. A more open democracy – with, for instance, laws guaranteeing freedom of information – which is closer to the people through devolution of power, would provide better safeguards against the abuses we have seen in recent years.

- Active citizens should be busy acquainting themselves with how our democracy works – or doesn't – and with the various proposals now on offer for reform – especially in the light of the introduction of closed party lists for European elections and the proposals for electoral reform outlined by Lord Jenkins in October 1998.

- Active citizens will want to take part in the institutions which govern our country – perhaps as a Justice of the Peace, school governor, local Councillor, MP or MEP.
- At the very least active citizens will want to understand fully how decisions affecting their lives are made.

It is not that we need to hack down our democratic system and start all over again: judicious pruning will effectively cut out the rotten areas and stimulate stronger growth.

Agenda for reform

Moving on from the question of vested interests, one of the principal reforms currently mooted is a change in the voting system – to reflect more accurately the opinions of the electorate. The basic argument – which I have helped to advance over the past 30 years – is that under the present system, governments are invariably elected with a minority of votes and their voting strength in Parliament does not reflect the votes cast for them in the country. Balanced against this unfairness, however, the 'first-past-the-post' system does have the advantage of being based on defined geographical constituencies so that theoretically MPs are accountable first and foremost to their constituents.

Representatives have become subservient to party machines. This is a great pity: in the past independent-minded MPs have often been the grit that produces the pearl in our parliamentary system.

In reality, political parties have wielded increasing political power in centrally selecting (and deselecting) MPs. The imposition of almost Trappist vows of silence on dissenting Labour MPs since the 1997 General Election and the exclusion of four Labour MEPs from the Parliamentary Labour Party because they would not sign a 'loyalty oath' are just two illustrations of the way in which representatives have become subservient to party machines. This is a great pity: in the past independent-minded MPs have often been the grit that produces the pearl in our parliamentary system.

I now sit as an Independent cross-bencher in the Upper House. This element of the House of Lords has a healthy disregard for such stifling party politics, and any reform of the Lords should seek to retain this independent streak – and not emasculate it by turning it into another preserve of party patronage.

The Lords needs to become more democratic without losing its ability to be more reflective and less adversarial than the Lower House. Abolishing hereditary peers and replacing them with party appointees, as Labour have mooted, would hardly represent progress. A model closer to the American Senate would be infinitely preferable. The value of the second chamber lies in its independence, in its ability to take a less partisan and longer view, and in its role as a check against the Lower House (often used effectively during the Thatcher Government). To create the biggest and best quango in Britain, with its red benches filled by party managers, does not suggest a politics which is being brought closer to the people.

When the people of Scotland and (by a much smaller margin) the people of Wales voted for a Scottish Parliament and a Welsh Assembly, they voted for bodies which would be elected by some form of proportionality. The next round of elections to the European Parliament are also meant to be fought using proportional representation, if the legislation goes through in time. Labour has a manifesto commitment to a referendum on proportional representation for Westminster (unless we are to be ridiculously over-governed, the House of Commons will need to be reduced in size by at least a third; there are far too many MPs). It is inconceivable that both Houses of the Westminster Parliament will not eventually be elected by some form of proportionality. But therein lies another conundrum: what form should this new voting system take?

The devil's in the detail

In politics the devil is always in the detail. There are any number of systems of proportional representation and understanding the details should matter to any citizen interested in the future of their democracy. What are the basic options?

It is inconceivable that both Houses of the Westminster Parliament will not eventually be elected by some form of proportionality.

- The various forms of national list (where MPs are centrally allocated by parties according to countrywide vote percentages) would completely sever the link between a constituency and an MP.

- A regional list system would be marginally more localized, but still favours 'party machine' politicians.

- The Australian system of alternative votes is not proportional, and puts greater power into the hands of the central party. This is the system which analysts say will most favour the Labour Party and, not surprisingly, many of their supporters are now arguing for this system.

- The single transferable vote cast in a multi-member constituency (often called community proportional representation) retains a relationship with a constituency while delivering a more proportional result. It also tends to militate against small extreme and unrepresentative groups (a danger with the list systems).

The Government wishes to introduce the 'closed party list system' for the 1999 European elections. For the first time ever, voters will not be able to vote for individual candidates – merely for the party of their choice – and seats will be allocated to the party's most favoured candidates on the basis of the votes cast. Different systems are proposed for the Scottish Parliament and Welsh Assembly, and for the Mayor of London.

Proportional systems can – but do not always – produce a less adversarial approach because political parties have to learn to work with one another.

This is a recipe for voter confusion. Complicated systems and the severing of the direct link between a voter and an elected representative are likely to create even more apathy. Who will bother to vote for a faceless cipher? The central party figures who will select the candidates will have even more power and the MEPs who are elected will be there because of the patronage of the party managers. This is a very unhealthy situation and will lead to even more authoritarian control over candidates and MPs.

None the less, change is vital. Careful thought and the right decision on the system will bring undoubted benefits. Proportional systems can – but do not always – produce a less adversarial approach because political parties have to learn to work with one another. In Britain a 'fair votes' system would certainly have the desirable effect of creating a more plural form of politics – prising off the straitjackets which currently constrain party members.

At present, if dissenters try to break out, the first-past-the-post system will almost certainly destroy them, whereas a more proportional system would allow for greater diversity. In 1983 the Liberal–SDP Alliance polled 25 per cent of the national vote (just 1 per cent less than Labour), but the electoral system delivered just 3 per cent of the seats to them. Socialists and Conservatives contemplating leaving their present parties know the the fate of the SDP and prefer to stay as reluctant inmates with a place in Parliament rather than face the risks associated with escape. But who can doubt that our present parties are unhappy coalitions in urgent need of realignment and renewal?

Devolving power

The voting system and the structure of our Westminster Parliament are not the only areas due to be overhauled. Scottish and Welsh devolution will also alter the balance of powers and encourage more subsidiarity. There is an increasing realization that the best bulwark against a European superstate is to entrench power at the lowest possible levels, in a 'Europe of regions'.

There is an increasing realization that the best bulwark against a European superstate is to entrench power at the lowest possible levels.

The European Parliament is a very inadequate check against a huge and largely unaccountable bureaucracy. It is widely believed that European bureaucracy goes its own sweet way and that the European Parliament should be given more effective powers of control (perhaps with an upper chamber, as Tony Blair has suggested). In fact, it is doubtful that the Parliament could ever discharge that function effectively. All the more reason, therefore, to devolve powers to local control and preserve regional and national identities. Europe will continue to flourish while power is radically dispersed and cultural diversity respected.

Such dispersal of power also points to a way of refocusing individual citizens' interest in civic matters through more localized opportunities for action. And Europe might cease to be the subject of such vituperation if the public believed it had become more accountable.

My early years in politics were spent in local government and I admit to a passion for local democracy. This is where 'ordinary people' often first become engaged in civic life. In recent years successive governments have adopted an attitude towards local government not dissimilar to that of Thomas Cromwell towards the monasteries in the sixteenth century: first list them, then ransack them, loot them and bust them, then confiscate all their assets. The destruction of local councils was accompanied by prescriptive legislation which stifled local decison-making. Many people declined to stand for election to the resulting rubber-stamp council chambers, and lost interest in local politics altogether.

The emasculation of local government and the absence of regional government has left Britain with one of the most centralized systems in Europe. The return of powers to local government, the establishment of regional government and of national government in Wales and Scotland, offer the antidote to this excessive centralization of power, and should encourage individual citizens to believe that their efforts can once again make a difference.

The emasculation of local government and the absence of regional government has left Britain with one of the most centralized systems in Europe.

I have already argued for a less secretive approach, for openness in public appointments, and for fewer quangos. This is just as relevant in the context of local government and in national government. Where quangos are unavoidable, the Public Accounts Committee of Parliament could be given wide-ranging powers, closer to the American Congressional model, to vet appointments and to investigate financial detail. More importantly, in the context of giving a voice back to local people, subsidiarity and the redistribution of power to the regions could undercut the quangos – and the recipients of political patronage who regularly populate them. So, too, could the direct election of more city mayors.

Mayors and local government

In my book *What Kind of Country?* I argued for a root and branch reform of local government.[6] I welcome Labour's decision to establish a directly elected mayor in London – and I hope that other cities will follow.

Local government also needs to be elected on a proportional basis if the people's voice is to be effectively heard.

When I looked at my American Internet listings for 'mayors' I was fascinated by the vibrant exchanges between incumbents and their challengers. This is the way in which local democracy is likely to develop in Britain. In the rest of Europe and in the USA, elected mayors give a focus for civic activity – and so long as they are given proper powers to hire and fire, they could bring considerable freshness to our local democracy.

Keeping it in proportion

Local government also needs to be elected on a proportional basis if the people's voice is to be effectively heard. The 1973 Royal Commission on Standards of Conduct in Political Life said that 'the local authorities most vulnerable to corruption have tended to be those in which one political party has unchallenged dominance'. This is another consequence of the first-past-the-post system. In Liverpool, for example, Militant Labour used the city as a battering ram for their political extremism for several years. Even at the height of their popularity they never obtained a majority of popular votes, but, like Mrs Thatcher's Government, with whom they were jousting, they enjoyed a majority of seats with a minority of votes. First-past-the-post breeds that kind of politics.

The single transferable vote keeps the best of our present system (MPs directly linked to constituents) but adds proportionality.

Faced with the unfairness of the first-past-the-post system and the authoritarian nature of closed party lists, voters might well lose heart and decide that it would probably be better to stick with 'the devil you know' rather than risk something worse. They would be wrong. The single transferable vote, which I have already described, keeps the best of our present system (MPs or councillors directly linked to constituents) but adds proportionality.

As the legislation passes through Westminster over the next couple of years, individual citizens will have the opportunity to grapple with these questions and should grab the chance to lobby their MPs and make sure that their views are heard. Although the options seem complex and hard to understand, more information is becoming available. Active citizens should campaign for more explanation from local or national government sources if necessary. Jenny Talbot of the Institute for Citizenship Studies has initiated a nationwide series of seminars, called 'Get the Vote Out', describing what changes are proposed and how the changes will impact on individual voters.

The cut and thrust

Politics will always involve some cut and thrust – and it is not a place for faint-hearts. My early experiences of local government gave me a passion for local democracy but not for some of its practices. The declaration of interests and the voting system are not the only areas of political life which desperately need to change. Rigged agendas, denial of free speech and political corruption were some of the least appetizing aspects of my time at a local level.

Politics will always involve some cut and thrust – and it is not a place for faint-hearts.

- At my first Council committee meeting – where I sat as the only member of my then party – the Chairman asked whether I had a seconder for a motion which I was seeking to move, even before he had heard my arguments. Predictably enough, no one was prepared to step out of line, the chairman simply brought down the gavel and moved on to the next item. And so it went on, until we managed to get someone else from the party elected who could then act as a seconder.

- Half the City Council got up and walked out when I made my maiden speech. I had challenged a planning decision to build a new housing development in an overspill area called Netherley. They were besotted with spine blocks, cluster blocks, walkways in the sky – planners' grandiose schemes and dreams which turned into nightmares for the uprooted people forced to live in them.

- One year later, in 1973, a party meeting was convened and my own party tried to expel me. Why? I had publicly questioned the role of a Liberal councillor in obtaining housing grants for properties which he owned. After an acrimonious battle, he resigned from the Council.

- Later, as deputy leader of the City Council, I had a chair thrown at me; the police had to intervene after a mob invaded the chamber and I was seized by the throat; on other occasions I had a brick in my face and the windows of my home daubed with white paint.

- Later still, in Parliament, episodes of hostility involved my weekly advice centres and my home being picketed, and my constituency offices being burnt out.

- As Housing Chairman, I said we should take some of the Vietnamese boat people as refugees and utilize some of our thousands of vacant properties to house them. Right-wingers circulated a fake letter, purportedly from me, to council tenants, telling them that refugees would be billeted with them. They were told to obtain blankets and to stock up with suitable foods. It produced the desired angry reaction. Merseyside local authorities nevertheless agreed to help nearly 1,000 refugees as a result of my comments.

I never expected it to be easy, but was perhaps unprepared at the beginning for the tough reality of speaking out against the majority, or on an unpopular issue. But don't be deterred: nothing will change if nothing is done, and your local community urgently needs the involvement of active, ethical and confident citizens. It is always worth getting involved. If you know your principles and stick with them, whatever is thrown at you, your efforts *will* make a difference.

Many times people have tried to bully me into voting this way or that or into shutting up. Whether it is the quick smear, the innuendo, or brazen appeals to self-advancement, some political operators have no qualms when it comes to manipulation. When I first entered Parliament my good friend Sir Cyril Smith told me to be my own man. He also reminded me that 'over there sits the opposition, and all around you are the enemy'. Anyone wanting to become active in politics should put their conscience first, then the interests of their constituents, their country, or their community – and only then the interests of their party.

Constitutional priorities

Giving priority to the right values is also a matter for close scrutiny as long overdue structural changes are made to our political system.

If executed in the right spirit, these changes will help renew our politics. The great danger is that the 'machine-men' of politics – the party managers and bosses – will use the opportunity to bolster their own positions and try to create a system that merely keeps the other side out.

Anyone wanting to become active in politics should put their conscience first, then the interests of their constituents, their country, or their community – and only then the interests of their party.

As we embark on a new constitutional settlement – questions which will dominate the 1997–2002 Parliament – citizens who take an active interest in the affairs of the nation will need to develop a mature view of these questions and not be content to leave them to the politicians. Organizations such as the Electoral Reform Society and Demos have produced practical information on what changes are afoot and what individual citizens can do about them.

At the end of the twentieth century, Britain needs a democracy which is up to the job of governing, one which is capable of delivering the sort of politics which its people want. At present we fool ourselves into believing that the mother of Parliaments is the envy of the world. It has its strengths and we should endeavour to hold onto the best of our system. As Conservative stubbornness over devolution in Scotland proved, however, constantly repeated refusals to change are not a substitute for reasoned, open argument and considered criticism. In the case of Scotland it led to the Party's annihilation. The present Tory leader William Hague does not seem alive to this weakness, simply reiterating more of the 'we will have no change' rhetoric.

There is little the Conservative Party can do from a position of such weakness to frustrate the changes which are now beginning to take shape. They should at least discharge their traditional role as guardians of our constitution by offering constructive criticism. In particular they risk being excluded from the debate about electoral reform because they have spent so long saying 'never' that they have little idea about the different variants on offer.

All parties and citizens need to have a clearer idea about the balance between rights and duties, and an informed view of the issues involved. Obligations are placed on us by virtue of our privilege of living in a free society. Democracies only flourish when their citizens believe in them and actively participate. A strong democracy remains the best bulwark against totalitarianism and dictatorship. It is also the best guarantor of peace: I know of no recorded case of two democracies declaring war on one another. More creative ways are found to resolve disputes. But if democracies are to flourish, they need to undergo a constant process of renewal.

Democracies only flourish when their citizens believe in them and actively participate.

Reform versus revolution

During the past two centuries in Britain our democratic rights have been systematically extended. At the end of the nineteenth century, in his original conclusion to his *Condition of the Working Class in England*, Engels wrote his famous prophecy:

> It is particularly easy to forecast future events in England because in that country every aspect of social development is so plain and clear-cut. The revolution *must* come. It is now too late for a peaceful outcome of the affair [i.e. the antagonism between the workers and the bourgeoisie] to be possible.[7]

Engels was spectacularly wrong about the inevitability of a Marxist revolution in Britain. This was in no small part due to the infinite capacity of the British throughout most of the past 200 years to undertake *reform*: to prune the tree rather than to fell it. Look at some of the great changes which have taken place during that time:

- The Reform Act of 1832
- The continued extension of the franchise throughout the nineteenth and early twentieth centuries
- The introduction of the secret ballot
- The 1911 Parliament Act reforming the House of Lords
- The response to the suffragette movement, giving voting rights to women

These are all examples of a capacity to bring about ordered change without resorting to the extremes of revolution. It is absurd, however, to pretend that this process of reform is now at an end. In every generation democracy must be reformed and renewed. A democracy which becomes set in concrete or fails to renew itself inevitably degenerates. It loses touch with people and, in turn, loses their confidence and their interest.

Reform and renewal

Among my own priorities to continue the process of reform and bring about a renewal of British democratic life would be the following action points:

- Legislation to make corrupting MPs a criminal offence
- A statutory requirement to declare all substantial individual donations to a political organization
- Access, via the Internet, and in every public library, to the MPs' Register of Financial Interests
- A requirement that all candidates publish details of their financial interests in election addresses

Reform of the way in which we hold MPs accountable would go some way towards restoring confidence in the individuals who govern us. This must be accompanied by a thorough-going reappraisal of the structures of government, leading to:

- A fairer system of voting – my personal preference is for one which through single transferable votes retains the link with a defined geographical area while producing a fairer and more representative result

- More open government – with the enactment of American-style freedom of information legislation
- Devolved regional government
- A reformed Upper House
- Reinvigorated local government

The new constitutional settlement must be undergirded by a renewed attitude on the part of every citizen, whether governed or governing.

- Every citizen can decide to participate actively in the way their country is run. Democracy is not for someone else: it is for all of us.
- Political parties should be more open to ideas from those they are serving, and less dependent on spin doctors, negative campaigning and sound-bites.
- Independent spirits in local and national government should be encouraged not suffocated.
- Somehow we need to resuscitate the ideal of public service.

Once the Liverpool John Moores University initiative to set up the Roscoe Lectures on Good Citizenship was under way, Professor Bernard Crick, the government adviser on the teaching of citizenship, told the all-party parliamentary group on citizenship that this approach was 'a good deed in a naughty world', and he wished other universities were 'as public spirited' in their approach. But most satisfactory of all, he said, was the sight of serious-minded citizens reclaiming their town hall and engaging in the complex question of what makes for good citizenship.

---

*Independent spirits should be encouraged
not suffocated.*

Reform and personal attitude

If one of the principal reasons why Marx and Engels were wrong about revolution in Britain is because they had no clear understanding of the capacity for self-reform, neither did they appreciate the critical role played by voluntary action and religious movements in preventing the development of an overwhelmingly militant working class. Britain does have an impressive record of public service.

Marx and Engels derided the Christian social ethic as a sham and ridiculed the concept of the common good as a distraction from class warfare. But religious revival touched every class in nineteenth-century Britain and the fact that there was no real parallel to this on the continent helps explain why Britain's politics took a different turn.

Voluntary organizations and campaigning groups first dirtied their own hands by meeting particular needs and then prevailed on the politicians to make provision on a statutory basis.

Active citizens of the time threw themselves into supporting every sort of reform and the century spawned an array of voluntary organizations and campaigning groups who first dirtied their own hands by meeting particular needs and then prevailed on the politicians to make provision on a statutory basis. This reached a crescendo in the social reforms of the Governments of 1906–14 and 1945–50. The creation of a welfare state and the extension of health and education to all regardless of their means were the products of these times. Fifty years on from the creation of the welfare state, precisely what proportion of the costs for these great innovations should be met by the individual and the state remains a controversial and current political question, but no one can dispute how these reforms first came about.

Frank Field and Tony Blair both see moral hazard in a system of welfare that appears to encourage cheating and idleness – though Field's departure from Blair's team does not augur well. At a lecture to honour the late Conservative politician and thinker Sir Keith Joseph, Field said that 'our welfare programme is … in part about

reinventing and nurturing civil society'. The architect of the 1945 reforms, William Beveridge, himself came to view state monopoly as
unhealthy. Total reliance on state handouts breeds inertia. Personal
endeavour must be encouraged and society (not just the Government)
must underpin the voluntary organizations. The notion of individual
and mutual responsibility is the backbone of community life.

In a society where we expect certain reciprocated
benefits, those who can must first
make a contribution.

An active citizen is one who will want to work. An obligation-based
view of citizenship will inevitably lead us to reject dependency and
to emphasize work as a necessary pillar of society. In a society where
we expect certain reciprocated benefits, those who can must first
make a contribution.

Reform and social action

At the beginning of the nineteenth century, when there was no
welfare state, voluntary efforts to relieve the suffering of the very
poor were spurred on by all branches of the Christian church.
Methodism's social ethic and Wesleyan modes of organization and
agitation were complemented by Evangelical and Catholic engagement in compassionate social action.

In Liverpool and Southwark, for example, young men went to
their graves suffering from cholera as they tried to serve the poor in
their parishes. Agitation for reform sprang from these harrowing experiences of deprivation and death. It began through letter-writing
and attempts to draw the public's attention to the horrors taking
place in their midst.

In a letter to *The Times*, dated 29 February 1832, three years after
Catholic Emancipation, Thomas Doyle wrote of the plight of his
congregation of some 20,000 souls in Southwark:

In mercy, as the friend of the suffering and deserted poor, do say something for the Irish poor of Southwark. Their terrible wretchedness (starving, sick, dying as they are) makes me in despair turn to you, that some generous souls may be acquainted with their forlorn state, and be moved to befriend them...

Many, many of these poor have no bed to lie on; they sleep at night on the floor without any other covering than the clothes – such as they are – which they have on them during the day. Others are almost in a state of nudity, and are compelled to keep within doors: these are poor widows with their destitute children...

It is not surprising that in a very unhealthy season like the present, many of these hapless people should sicken and die: the wonder is how they live at all, under so many privations and extreme suffering.[8]

The editor of *The Times* opened an appeal and several months later, on 22 June 1832, he was able to report that some of the worst suffering had been relieved.

A more systematic approach was taken by Evangelicals who created a whole tradition of philanthropic humanitarianism. William Wilberforce and his allies helped to secure the abolition of slavery, while Lord Shaftesbury's multitude of reforming campaigns led him to fight against inhumanity in the factories and the mines, the employment of children as chimney sweeps, the treatment of mentally ill people, against inadequate public health, poor housing and the absence of drains. Through legislative and voluntary action – the latter usually spawning the former – these were mammoth strides in humanizing a dehumanized economic order and the abased society which it had created.

Middle-class philanthropy too seldom questioned the actual structure and organization of society.

While Marx and Engels gravely underestimated the impact of this flurry of voluntary and legislative reform, they were right in their perception that middle-class philanthropy too seldom questioned the actual structure and organization of society. This is best illustrated by the support of William Wilberforce for the government's actions at Peterloo (when, in Manchester, they brutally suppressed a meeting of people calling for emancipation) and by Shaftesbury's decision to vote against the extension of the suffrage proposed in the Reform Bills of 1832 and 1867.

In our own times, organizations such as the Greens have raised considerable public awareness of environmental issues, and countless groups and individuals work tirelessly to help the underprivileged, or give time to support any number of good causes. As with some cases in the nineteenth century, however, an increased awareness about single issues has not always translated itself into fully fledged political action. Hundreds of thousands of people will enthusiastically take part in a Countryside Movement protest about the destruction of rural England, for example, but how many will translate this into political action via the ballot box?

Reform and political action

Later in the nineteenth century the Nonconformist thinker and Liberal intellectual Professor T.H. Green created a rigorous political creed – Idealism – to give consistency and logic to the impetus of all the voluntary and charitable activity. Charles Loch and Arnold Toynbee were among those who fell under Green's spell. Meanwhile, Cardinal Manning and Charles Booth mobilized the poor, organizing street protests and local projects, and meeting people personally where they lived and worked. Booth estimated that in London 30 per cent of the population lived at or below the level of subsistence. Loch summed up the new creed of activism thus: 'The new charity requires of the rich, that, for the common good, they submit to the common yoke of labour and that they help the poor to become self-dependent and competent fellow citizens.'

If the state wants fully formed citizens, it cannot afford to have an outcast or excluded underclass. Therefore the state must address the causes of poverty.

Pauperism and cycles of poverty and dependency are the enemy of the modern state. If the state wants fully formed citizens, it cannot afford to have an outcast or excluded underclass. Therefore, Green argued, the state must understand the causes of poverty and take practical action – through the tax and benefit system – to alleviate the problem. This is still a need now, at the end of the twentieth century.

For their part, individual citizens today can follow Green's active creed and help out in voluntary projects in deprived neighbourhoods (such as the service learning initiatives described in Chapter 3), or in social investment and credit union projects (outlined in Chapter 2), or in campaigns on issues such as solving debt problems (there is one being run at present by the Jubilee 2000 group).

In 'Political Obligation' Green identified the laws which he said had to be reformed as those which 'check the development of the moral disposition'. Among these were 'laws which interfere with the growth of self-reliance, with the formation of a manly conscience and sense of moral dignity … legal institutions which take away the occasion for the exercise of certain moral virtues (e.g. the Poor Law which takes away the occasion for the exercise of parental fore-thought, filial reverence and neighbourly kindness).'[9]

Green knew that, left to themselves, certain individuals and groups will never do what is required for the good of themselves and their children, and so they must be compelled to do so. This attitude is anathema to the modern libertarian, of course, but Green held that we must take people as they are to make them into what they should be.

We must take people as they are to make them into what they should be.

Green was an acute political thinker, but he was also a great activist, engaging in all the issues of the day. At Oxford he addressed the 'town and gown' divide by becoming the first don to sit on the City Council. He campaigned for temperance – stressing the primacy of the inner checks and balances essential to the good person and the good citizen. He championed the cause of education, sitting on Oxford's school board, personally contributing to the building of a grammar school, founding a scholarship for boys from elementary schools, providing a house at Balliol for students with financial difficulties, and promoting adult education, especially through the University Extension Movement. He was also the first secretary of the Association for the Higher Education of Women. When he died, it was his wish to be buried in the North Ward of Oxford which he had represented. Citizenship, he had strongly believed, had to be practised through activity as well as taught.

A new contract

Green's Idealism largely disappeared in the mud of the Somme. After World War I harsher and more ideological (i.e. Socialist) political creeds came to dominate. But it is possible to see in the approach of modern politicians such as Frank Field and Chris Patten the same urge to champion work and personal responsibility alongside the continuing availability of state help for genuine need.

If we simply wait for someone else to act, we are abdicating our very right to call ourselves citizens.

Field despises the 'citizenship' of the past 40 years – which has measured citizenship, if at all, in terms of entitlements and pursued the belief that equality must be sought through the dispensing of ever more welfare. Frank Field (and others like him) is genuinely horrified by the cycles of dependency and fraud which have displaced the promotion of civil community and the encouragement of families as a primary source of support.

What is needed more than anything else is a thorough-going review of citizenship. *Everyone* should be actively involved in this. The new welfare reforms will not succeed without a reworking of what is expected of the citizen: they will simply appear to most people as harsh, punitive measures forced on them by an uncaring state. If, however, the reforms could be part of a new contract between the citizen and the state, based on *reciprocal* duties and rights, responsibilities and entitlements, then they could be the most important social change of the last half-century.

To make this change, we will all need to play a far more active part in the diverse institutions and organizations which make up the life of our nation. If we simply wait for someone else to act, we are abdicating our very right to call ourselves citizens.

Essential Questions

- Are you willing to take positive action to support a cause that concerns you – by joining a pressure group, a voluntary organization, a professional body, or a trade union?

- Is there a need in your area to start a campaign for more amenities or community facilities? Could you do this? Could you encourage someone else to do it?

- Could you be active in a political party?

- Have you ever written to or lobbied your local Councillor, MP or MEP? Do you know how to go about it?

- How much do you know about the proposed changes to the voting system? Do you understand how they will affect you?

- Would you consider standing for election yourself?

- Have you thought about taking on a formal 'service' role, as a JP, prison visitor or school governor, or as an officer of a local charity, voluntary group, tenants' or residents' association?

- How seriously do you take your duty to vote in elections?

- Do you think that all forms of 'active citizenship' are not for you and should be left to someone else?

- If you have believed this in the past, are you ready to think again and get out and get involved?

Conclusion

We face some hard challenges today as we work to shape our personal and political priorities. Life in the modern world is complex; we are surrounded by confusing issues where right and wrong are not always crystal clear; we can see severe social problems all around us, and the need for change in many areas is obvious. Above all, there is an urgent need for people to focus less on themselves as individuals – what will benefit me? – and more on the common good – what will benefit the whole community? If we have the confidence to form our own ideas and principles, we can choose our causes and start to act as effective citizens in our community, through campaign organizations, local groups, single issue groups, charitable work, voluntary organizations, political movements and parties, professional associations and trades unions.

First of all, though, we need to develop a clear understanding of what is involved and what is at stake. Being able to vote, under whatever system, is an essential condition for participation in our democracy. But real involvement goes deeper than that. In this book I have tried to set out what it means to be a citizen – the issues we all need to understand, and the rights and duties involved.

Aristotle held that there was something innate about a citizen's desire to take part in public life, and his ideas, formed so long ago, are just as relevant for us today. His concept of *koinonia*, the community, was not about structures of government but about the qualities in mankind which made civic co-existence a possibility. Man alone, he argued, had the *logos*, the ability to speak, but more than that, we have the ability to use reason and to act as moral agents. 'It is a characteristic of man,' he said, 'that he alone has any sense of good and evil, of just and unjust.'[1]

Aristotle's *polis* (city/state) was 'an association of free men' which governed itself; where citizens would 'take turn to govern and be governed' – a familiar notion for the modern democrat always expectant of losing or winning public office.

Active citizenship does not just happen.
Education is essential.

The *polis* was also the school of life. Each citizen would be formed through knowledge and experience of its laws, religion, traditions, festivals and culture and through participation in its common institutions. Its architecture, its theatre (the nearest equivalent in Athenian society to our concept of a free press: particularly in plays which dared to satirize and to explore controversial questions), its orators, its laws: all were manifestations of the common life and all required the commitment of its citizens.

It was a duty, an obligation, to engage in the *polis*, sharing in both the burdens and the glories. A person who withdrew from the *polis* was vilified, as participation in the life of the city was seen as crucial to each individual's full development. This ancient wisdom is worth bearing in mind as we consider the dismal turnout in many British elections. What are we allowing ourselves to miss out on by not taking part?

Active citizenship does not just happen, however. Education is essential – beginning in our homes and continuing in our schools and colleges. All citizens need to be taught to appreciate the needs of the whole community, and how to accommodate the general will where possible (although there will be times when it is right to stand against the majority view). As well as knowing that we have certain rights as citizens, we also need to understand our responsibilities to the wider community, and we must be prepared to serve that community by informing ourselves about issues, casting our votes, working for the common good and, if necessary, fighting for the community and its democratic institutions.

All men and women should be treated as
ends, never as means.

Such active citizenship can be lived out at a local level, in regional government, in central government at Westminster, or in the European Parliament. It is probably at the local level that most people will first learn that all men and women should be treated as ends, never as means. That is what the 'common good' is all about. We should always be suspicious of partisanship and political scheming that seeks to delocalize politics or to uncouple the people from the workings (and therefore the benefits) of their own democracy.

The nineteenth-century French politician de Tocqueville remarked that an impressive practical wisdom and power of judgement may be developed simply from participating in the affairs of a free society. There is no substitute for experience learnt at the coal-face of democracy. Academic theories have their place, but better than all the theories and teaching combined are the practical actions which we take as citizens. It is crucially important just to take part.

The politicians I most admire are those who have specific causes and ideas. I wonder about those who do not. Why are they in politics if not to pursue causes or explore ideas? If a man or woman has an idea or a cause which they seek to realize, they become idealists and motivated reformers. Politics today needs both of these. The reformer has the moral initiative and courage to challenge the status quo and to bring a cause to the attention of the nation. Reform, rather than the violence and destruction of revolution, implies steady progress towards an ethical ideal. Ideals are most often realized by being championed through specific causes.

The combination of ethics, reform and idealism is the sure foundation for active, effective citizenship – and Cicero said that the glory of activity is that it leads to virtue.

It is crucially important just to take part.

CITIZEN VIRTUES

how you can make a difference

AT HOME

- Pass on positive values to your children – respect for others and themselves, self-discipline, the value of work and education, how to say 'no' when pressured to do something wrong.
- Set clear boundaries of behaviour. Don't be afraid to give firm but loving guidance.
- Set the best example you can, and don't give up when you fail.
- Keep in close touch with relatives – maintain the extended family as a mutual support system.
- Pay particular attention to elderly relatives or neighbours – visit them with your children.
- Resolve to do whatever it takes to create a stable family life.
- Choose carefully what you and your children watch on television, video or in the cinema.
- Regulate the computer games your children play, and access to the Internet.
- Read to your children as much as possible – and encourage them to develop their ideas, imagination and communication skills.
- Make family conversation and activities a priority. Spend time on your children.
- Be prepared to have open family discussions on topics which come up in the news, or on issues such as drugs, crime, violence, abortion, etc. Allow your children to air their own views and decide what they think.
- Decide as a family to recycle whatever you can, and make a habit of using environmentally friendly products around the home.

- Agree a family policy on ethical investments, including mortgage and pensions, and try to use individual shareholder power to push for change in companies following unethical practices.

- Adopt a charity or cause which you can support as a family – preferably with both money and time.

AT SCHOOL
PARENTS

- Make sure that your children are getting the essential education they need at the right time – particularly literacy and numeracy skills.

- Check up on the reading material they are being given. Parents *and* teachers should both demand that only top-quality, positive books are on the curriculum. Campaign strongly against the use of texts you feel are inappropriate.

- Campaign for a return to 'value-added' rather than 'value-neutral' education. Young people need guidance and an ethical foundation.

- Find out what is being done in your local school to educate for citizenship – and demand changes if this is not being done.

TEACHERS/GOVERNORS

- Find ways to develop your pupils' self-confidence. Encourage them to articulate their thoughts and hold on confidently to personal values.

- Hold classroom debates on ethical issues and politics as part of the teaching process.

- If the basics of democracy and community values are not being taught in your school, get a discussion going on how it might be achieved.

- Set up a service learning project, or other initiative whereby pupils can take part in voluntary work as part of the community.

- Establish a good citizenship award within the school.

- Be aware of bullying and criminal pressures within your school. Do what you can to stop it; encourage open discussion on such issues in the classroom; make sure that pupils know they can talk to an adult privately about a problem; prepare pupils to stand up against such pressures and to protect each other.

- Make sure that clear, sensible teaching is given to all pupils about sex, drugs, smoking and alcohol.

AT WORK

- Think of ways your company could be more flexible in terms of working hours or job sharing to benefit working parents. There may be scope to improve on company policy regarding maternity and paternity leave.

- Be aware of your company's place in the community. Suggest or carry out ideas for local interaction – e.g. special employment projects, local investment, or sponsorship of amenities or school initiatives.

- Adopt a company charity.

- Whatever your position in the company, give proper consideration to ethical issues and act accordingly – including honesty and transparency in business dealings; recycling possibilities; employee conditions; human rights issues in foreign supplier companies; investment policies and company pension schemes.

- Join a trade union or professional body and become actively involved with the issues it is promoting or questioning, including working conditions and practices, fair wages, etc.

- Investigate the possibilities for your company to get involved in employment projects for young school-leavers – including work experience, training schemes, apprenticeships and full-time positions.

- Speak out if you believe something is fundamentally wrong with your company's policies or practices.

- If your company needs to lobby Parliament on an issue, gather information and go directly through your local MP to reach the Minister.

IN THE COMMUNITY

- How well do you know your neighbours? Talk to the people on your street and see if you can get some community spirit going – a street party, perhaps, or helping each other out with gardening or DIY.

- Have a particular care for elderly neighbours – are they being looked after properly? Are they lonely? Make the time to visit and help out if you can.

- Pick a local charity, support group, campaigning or voluntary organization to support, and give not only money but time – e.g. youth group, single mothers' support group, hospice, drug rehabilitation centre, residents' association, Age Concern centre, elderly residents' visiting scheme.

- Set up/campaign for/join a local credit union initiative, or service learning project, or a neighbours' service-swapping scheme.

- Get involved with your local schools, as a parent or a governor, and encourage the setting up of citizenship projects and voluntary work for the pupils.

- Inform yourself about local concerns and needs. Contact those involved with questions and suggestions.

- Keep in touch with events in your local newspaper or village magazine; go to residents' or council meetings when you can – don't leave community affairs to 'the usual crowd'.

- Shop ethically – choose one product over another for environmental or human rights reasons. Vote with your feet and your cash, and encourage local shops to stock the products you are prepared to buy.

- Make the most of local recycling facilities and encourage neighbours to do the same.

IN POLITICS

- If you feel strongly about a particular issue, stand for election to local or national government and make your voice heard as a representative of your community.
- Join the local branch of the political party you support and take an active part in their meetings and campaigns.
- At the very least lobby your MP or question election candidates and local Councillors on issues which concern you – e.g. housing, support for the family, investment policies, local amenities, honesty in public life, arms sales, education, youth crime, drug legislation, abortion, euthanasia, etc.
- Question your local government representatives on the Council's investment policies – make sure they are giving due weight to ethical considerations.
- Attend meetings on local issues: your view is as valid as anyone else's.
- Before voting look closely at the declared interests of all election candidates and their record of honesty or otherwise in public life. Make sure you are fully informed before making your choice. Refuse to vote for any candidate who appears to have conflicting interests or a less than clean public record.
- Take the trouble to vote at every opportunity, in both local and national elections, including referenda. It is your democratic right and your vote can make a difference.
- If you are active in other ways in support of a particular cause (e.g. countryside protection), make sure that your vote reflects your opinions.

- Use your vote wisely. Inform yourself before voting about all the parties and candidates. Question the candidates who visit about their policies on issues of local and national concern.
- Make sure you understand the incoming constitutional and electoral reforms (i.e. devolution and proportional voting) so that you will know how to use your vote when the time comes.

Notes

Introduction

1. Oliver James, *Britain On the Couch*, Century, 1997.
2. Francis Fukuyama, *The End of Order*, The Social Market Foundation, 1997.
3. T.H. Green, *Prolegomena To Ethics*, Oxford University, Clarendon Press, 1883.

Chapter 1

1. John Stuart Mill, *On Liberty*, Longman, 1864 (3rd ed.), chapter 5.
2. Alisdair MacIntyre, *After Virtue: A Study in Moral Theory*, Duckworth, 1981.
3. Ian Mitroff and Warren Bennis, *The Unreality Industry*, Carol Publishing Group, 1989.
4. Bruce Gyngell, in an address to the Royal Television Society, London, 19 June 1996, quoted in the *Daily Mail* and *Guardian*, 20 June 1996.
5. Professor Gerald Caplan, 'Preventing psychological problems in children of divorce: general practitioners' role' in *British Medical Journal* (clinical research edition), 31 May 1986, vol. 292, pp. 1431–4; and 'Preventing psychological problems in children of divorce: guidelines for general practitioners' in *BMJ*, 14 June 1986, vol. 293, pp. 1563–6.
6. Monica Cockett and John Tripp, *The Exeter Family Study: Family breakdown and its impact on children*, University of Exeter Press, 1994.
7. A.H. Halsey, *Children and Society*, Nuffield College, Oxford, 1993.
8. Allan Bloom, *The Closing of the American Mind*, Simon & Schuster, 1987.
9. Melanie Phillips, *All Must Have Prizes*, Little, Brown & Co., 1996.
10. Cited in Norman Dennis, *Who's Celebrating What?*, Christian Institute, 1995.

11. Edmund Leach, Reith Lectures, 1967.

12. Rob Parsons, *Sixty Minute Father*, Hodder & Stoughton, 1995.

Chapter 2

1. John Ruskin, *Sesame and Lilies*, Smith, Elder & Co., 1865.

2. *The Ethical Consumer*, Oct/Nov 1997.

3. Russell Sparkes, *The Ethical Investor*, HarperCollins, 1995.

4. Charles Jacob, in Sparkes, *The Ethical Investor*.

5. Phil White, in *Financial Adviser*, 25 September 1997.

6. 'You can have your cake and eat it', report by the WM Company, 1997.

7. Mallin, Saadouni and Briston, 'The Financial Performance of Ethical Investment Funds', in the *Journal of Business Finance and Accounting*, June 1995.

8. Letter to the author, January 1998.

9. Sparkes, *The Ethical Investor*.

10. Robert D. Klassen and Curtis P. McLaughlin, 'The impact of environmental management on firm performance', *Journal of Management Science*, August 1996, vol. 42, no. 8.

11. *Financial Exclusion*, UKSIF, 1997.

12. *Hansard* (House of Commons), 9 July 1997, col. 855.

Chapter 3

1. Luke Harding, John Salmon and Cathy Scott Clark, 'Fury at gang rape lessons', *Sunday Express*, 16 May 1993.

2. Cassandra Jardine, 'Teenage terror with a purpose', *Daily Telegraph*, 5 October 1994.

3. *Daily Mail*, 26 April 1994.

4. Dr James Dobson, *Discipline While You Can*, Kingsway, 1978.

5. C.S. Lewis, *The Abolition of Man*, Collins, Fount Paperbacks, 1943.

6. Matthew Arnold, *Culture and Anarchy*, Smith, Elder & Co., 1869.

7. Department for Education and Employment, *Excellence in Schools* (Cm. 3681), HMSO, 1997.

8. David Alton, 'Our first classes of citizens', *The Times*, 10 July 1997.

9. Lewis Mumford, *The City of History*, Pelican, 1961.

10. Ibid.

11. H.G. Wells, *World Brain*, Methuen, 1938.
12. Edmund Burke, 'A Letter to a Member of the National Assembly', 1791, in *The Works of the Right Honourable Edmund Burke*, London, 1792–1827.
13. Burke, 'Letters on a Regicide Peace', 1796, ibid.
14. Peter Ackroyd, *The Life of Thomas More*, Chatto & Windus, 1998.
15. *Idea*, Evangelical Alliance, January 1995.
16. I have written about him more extensively in *Signs of Contradiction*, Hodder & Stoughton, 1996.
17. Ramsay Muir, *History of Liverpool*, Liverpool University Press, 1907.
18. Material available from the Foundation for Citizenship at Liverpool John Moores University, Roscoe Court, 4 Rodney Street, Liverpool L1 2TZ.

Chapter 4

1. *What On Earth Are We Doing To Our Children?*, Maranatha, 109 Irlam Road, Flixton, Manchester, 1997.
2. *Readers Digest*, July 1994.
3. *The Times*, 8 April 1994.
4. G.K. Chesterton, *The Man Who Was Thursday*, J.W. Arrowsmith, 1908.

Chapter 5

1. *Guardian*, 3 October 1996.
2. Leonard Hobhouse, 'Liberalism', in *Liberalism & Other Writings*, James Meadowcroft (ed.), Cambridge University Press, 1994.
3. Jacques Maritain, *Christianity & Democracy*, Geoffrey Bles, 1945.
4. *Royal Commission on Standards of Conduct in Public Life* (Chairman: The Rt Hon. The Lord Salmon), Cmnd. 6524, HMSO, 1976.
5. *Hansard* (House of Commons), 2 April 1990, col. 393 (Written Answers).
6. David Alton, *What Kind of Country?* Marshall Pickering, 1988.
7. Friedrich Engels, *Condition of the Working Class in England*, 1892, trans. and ed. W.O. Hendeson and W.H. Chaloner, Oxford, Basil Blackwell, 1958.
8. Quoted in *The Great Link*, Canon Bernard Dogan, Burns & Oates, 1948.

9. T.H. Green, *Political Obligation,* in *The Works of T.H. Green*, R.L. Nettleship (ed.), 3 vols, London, Longmans, 1885–8.

Conclusion

1. Aristotle, 'Politics', Book I, Chapter 2, in *The Complete Works of Aristotle*, Jonathan Barnes (ed.), Princeton University Press, 1984, vol. 2.

Select Bibliography

Acland, Arthur H. Dyke, *The Education of Citizens*, Manchester, Central Cooperative Board, 1883

Bryce, James, *The Hindrances to Citizenship*, New Haven, Yale, 1909

Crowe, Ian (ed.), *Edmund Burke: His Life And Legacy*, London, Four Courts Press, 1997

Etzioni, Amitai, *The Spirit of Community*, New York, Crown Publishers, 1993

Fisher, H.A.L., *The Common Weal*, Oxford, Clarendon Press, 1924

Green, T.H., *Prolegomena To Ethics*, Oxford, Clarendon Press, 1883

Jones, Sir Henry, *The Principles of Citizenship*, London, Macmillan, 1919

MacCunn, John, *Ethics of Citizenship*, Glasgow, J Maclehose & Sons, 1894

Maritain, Jacques, *Christianity & Democracy*, London, Geoffrey Bles, 1945

Nettleship, R.L. (ed.), *The Works of T.H. Green*, 3 vols, London, Longmans, 1885–8

Phillips, Melanie, *All Must Have Prizes*, London, Little Brown & Co., 1996.

Richter, Melvin, *The Politics of Conscience: T.H. Green and his Age*, London, Weidenfeld & Nicholson, 1964

Sacks, Jonathan, *Faith In The Future*, London, Darton, Longman & Todd, 1995

Sacks, Jonathan, *The Politics of Hope*, London, Jonathan Cape, 1997

Selbourne, David, *The Principle of Duty*, London, Sinclair Stevenson, 1994